OURARTOU
URARTU

In the same series:

ANATOLIA I   U. Bahadır Alkım, Professor at the University of
(From the beginnings to the end   Istanbul
of the 2nd millennium B.C.)

ANATOLIA II   Henri Metzger, Professor at the University of Lyons
(1st millennium B.C.)

BYZANTIUM   Antoine Bon, Professor at the University of Lyons

CELTS AND GALLO-ROMANS   Jean-Jacques Hatt, Professor at the University of
                                    Strasbourg

CENTRAL AMERICA   Claude Baudez, Research Professor at the Centre
                                    National de Recherches Scientifiques (C.N.R.S.), Paris

CENTRAL ASIA   Aleksandr Belenitsky, Professor at the Archaeological
                                    Institute of Leningrad

CHINA

CRETE   Nicolas Platon, former Superintendent of Antiquities,
                                    Crete; Director of the Acropolis Museum, Athens

CYPRUS   Vassos Karageorgis, Director of the Archaeological
                                    Museum, Nicosia

EGYPT   Jean Leclant, Professor at the Sorbonne, Paris

THE ETRUSCANS   Raymond Bloch, Professor at the Sorbonne, Paris

GREECE I   Nicolas Platon, former Superintendent of Antiquities,
(Mycenaean and geometric periods)   Crete; Director of the Acropolis Museum, Athens

GREECE II   François Salviat, Professor at the University of Aix-
(Post-geometric periods)   en-Provence

INDIA   Maurizio Taddei, Inspector of Oriental Art and Ar-
                                    chaeology, Rome

INDOCHINA   Bernard P. Groslier, Curator of Historical Monu-
                                    ments, Angkor; Director of Archaeological Research
                                    at the Ecole Française d'Extrême-Orient

INDONESIA   Bernard P. Groslier, Curator of Historical Monu-
                                    ments, Angkor; Director of Archaeological Research
                                    at the Ecole Française d'Extrême-Orient

MESOPOTAMIA	Jean-Claude Margueron, Agrégé of the University; Member of the French Institute of Archaeology of Beirut
MEXICO	Jacques Soustelle
PERSIA I (From the origins to the Achaemenids)	Jean-Louis Huot, Agrégé of the University; Member of the French Institute of Archaeology of Beirut
PERSIA II (From the Seleucids to the Sassanians)	Vladimir Lukonin, Curator at the Hermitage Museum, Leningrad
PERU	Rafael Larco Hoyle †, Director of the Rafael Larco Herrera Museum, Lima
PREHISTORY	Denise de Sonneville-Bordes, Ph. D.
ROME	Gilbert Picard, Professor at the Sorbonne, Paris
SOUTH CAUCASUS	Boris B. Piotrovsky, Director of the Hermitage Museum, Leningrad
SOUTH SIBERIA	Mikhail Gryaznov, Professor at the Archaeological Institute of Leningrad
SYRIA-PALESTINE I (Ancient Orient)	Jean Perrot, Head of the French Archaeological Mission in Israel
SYRIA-PALESTINE II (Classical Orient)	Michael Avi Yonah, Professor at the Hebrew University of Jerusalem
THE TEUTONS	R. Hachmann, Professor at the University of Saarbrücken

ANCIENT
CIVILIZATIONS

Series prepared under the direction
of Jean Marcadé, Professor of Archaeology
at the University of Bordeaux

THE ANCIENT CIVILIZATION OF

URARTU

BORIS B. PIOTROVSKY

Translated from the Russian by JAMES HOGARTH

69 illustrations in colour; 59 illustrations in black and white

COWLES BOOK COMPANY, INC.
488 MADISON AVENUE
NEW YORK, N.Y. 10022

CONTENTS

Preface 9

Introduction 11

Chapter I   *The Rediscovery of Urartu* 13
             From Moses Khorenatsi to Friedrich Schulz 13
             The Museums make their First Acquisitions 15
             Treasure-Hunters and Clandestine Diggers 16
             The Beginnings of Archaeology in Central Urartu . . 18
             The Exploration of Soviet Armenia 21
             Recent Research in Turkey 24
             Progress and Prospects 38

Chapter II   *The Problem of Origins* 41
             Early Cultures in Armenia 41
             Uruatri and Nairi in the Second Millennium B.C. . . . 43
             The Campaigns of Shalmaneser III and the Balawat
             Gates 45
             The Urartian Kingdom in the 9th Century B.C. . . . 48
             The Rise of Urartu 50

Chapter III   *History and Archaeology* 65
             The First Great Reigns 65
             Erebuni and Argishtihinili 69
             Urartu and Assyria in the 8th Century B.C. 72
             The Reign of Rusa I 83
             The Archives of the Assyrian Secret Service 86
             Sargon's Campaign against Urartu 88
             Urartian Works of Art in Sargon's Booty 112
             Argishti II and the Recovery of Urartu: the Finds at
             Altıntepe 125
             Assyria in Difficulties: the Reign of Rusa II 128
             Building Activity in Urartu in the 7th Century B.C. . . . 132

Chapter IV   The City of Teisheba (Karmir-Blur)   135
             The Site and the Excavations   135
             Workshops and Store-Rooms   138
             The Name of the Fortress   153
             Stock-Rearing and Animal Sacrifices   154
             Records and Inscriptions   157
             Other Finds   173
             Influences and Connections   175
             Layout of the Town   177
             The Destruction of Teishebaini   178
             Conclusion   193

Chapter V   Epilogue   195
             The Last Kings of Urartu   195
             The Decline of Assyria and the Rise of the Scythians .   197

Chronological Table   201

Bibliography   203

List of Illustrations   209

Index   219

PREFACE

*I*t is right that a volume on Ancient Civilizations *should be devoted to Urartu, since this is a relatively recent province of the vast domain of contemporary archaeology. The historical importance to which the Kingdom of Van attained in the first half of the first millennium B.C. was totally forgotten until in the 19th century attention was directed to this area in Armenia by the accounts of a traveller and the discovery by clandestine diggers of numbers of bronze objects of remarkable quality; and it is only within the last thirty years or so that methodical exploration has been undertaken, supplying new epigraphic evidence to confirm and supplement Assyrian sources and to reveal the remains of Urartian civilisation, often astonishingly well preserved, on the sites of ancient fortresses.*

But Urartu is also of particular interest and relevance to our survey of the different aspects of archaeology throughout the world.

First, in relation to the problems *of archaeology—how they first presented themselves, how they were formulated and approached by archaeologists, with some fumblings and hesitations, and how they were then set in their proper perspective in the history of the civilisations of the Middle East—the author of this book has much of interest to tell us.*

From the point of view of archaeological methods, *too, it is instructive to read in this book how Urartian inscriptions can be used to amplify and correct the Assyrian annals, and to consider the important contribution made by archaeological material when the written sources are scanty or too evidently reflect dynastic policy: on social and economic life and on cultural contacts, for example, our most concrete knowledge is derived from excavation.*

And finally, of course, while the results *of archaeological exploration depend largely on the conditions offered by the site, they also depend on the selection of the right techniques, the application of rigorous scientific method and the correctness of the conclusions drawn. In this respect an excavation like*

9

Karmir-Blur is of great exemplary value, and undoubtedly represents an advance towards that "integral resurrection of the past" sought by Michelet, still the ideal and the dream of every archaeologist.

We also owe a debt of particular gratitude to Mr Boris Piotrovsky for enriching his text with such a magnificent choice of illustrations, selected from the treasures of the splendid museum of which he is Director and the Historical Museum of Erevan.

J. M.

We should like to express our very sincere thanks to the author, Professor Boris B. Piotrovsky, who devoted himself wholeheartedly to compiling this work, made available first-hand material at Leningrad and in Armenia, and generously put at our disposal his invaluable experience as Director of the Karmir-Blur excavations for over twenty years.

We are also grateful to Mr V. Meliksetyan, Director of the Armenian Historical Museum at Erevan and to all his collaborators: Messrs K. Kafadaryan, V. Gazazyan, Mrs E. Gevorkyan and Mrs Karapetyan, Messrs P. Grigoryan, T. Khachatryan, R. Ovannesyan and S. Esayan, who gave us much kind help and advice during our stay.

INTRODUCTION

Time has dealt in different ways with the kingdoms of the past. The fame of some of them has resounded through the ages; the memory of men has preserved the names of their kings, their triumphs and achievements; and their buildings have survived the centuries and are correctly credited to those who built them. The chroniclers recorded their history, which has been handed down orally from generation to generation and copied and recopied in many languages from age to age. This was the case, for example, with Egypt, Babylonia, Assyria, Greece, Rome and many other nations of antiquity. But elsewhere the situation was very different. A kingdom which had known its period of greatness and then declined would sink into total oblivion; the achievements of its rulers, such of its buildings as were spared by the passage of time, and even its oral traditions would be ascribed to other nations, often enough to the very nations which had been its enemies; and it would disappear for many centuries from human consciousness. This was the fate of Urartu, a kingdom which developed in the mountainous area round Lake Van, on the territory of present-day Turkey, and became a powerful force in western Asia between the 9th and the 7th centuries B.C. Then, early in the 6th century, the kingdom of Urartu was overthrown and soon afterwards forgotten, in the turmoil which accompanied the formation of new nations and new kingdoms in the territory which it had controlled.

THE REDISCOVERY OF URARTU

I

From Moses Khorenatsi to Friedrich Schulz

For three centuries Urartu was a formidable rival to Assyria. Though twice defeated by the Assyrians, the Urartians several times prevailed in this contest, and indeed—though only by a few decades—outlasted their rivals. But posterity dealt harshly with the memory of Urartu. The name was preserved in the Old Testament in the corrupt form "Ararat", which in the Latin version became "Armenia". When the Massoretic writers were vocalising the text of the Bible they inserted the vowel *a* into words which were unknown to them, so that "Urartu" became "Ararat"; and it is only within very recent years that the Qumran scrolls have yielded a form of the name with the semi-vowel *w* in the first syllable.

By an irony of fate, oral tradition and the writings of mediaeval historians ascribed the surviving works of the Urartians to their rivals the Assyrians. Thus Moses Khorenatsi, an Armenian historian of the 5th century, attributed the building of the large city of which remains still survived on a crag on the shores of Lake Van to the Assyrian Queen Samiram (Semiramis). He relates how she brought together twelve thousand labourers and six thousand skilled craftsmen from Assyria and its tributary countries, and ". . . within a few years had completed this most wondrous work, with mighty walls and gates of brass. In the town itself she built a great number of splendid buildings, showing much variety in the use of stone and in colouring, of two and three stories, some of them with balconies. Most skilfully she planned the town, with handsome wide streets. . . On its outskirts to the east, the north and the south she laid out farmsteads and shady groves of fruit-trees and other leafy trees, and planted many flourishing gardens and vineyards. Many other fine things she brought to pass in the city, and settled in it great numbers of citizens. But all the splendours which she created in the upper part of the city were inaccessible to the general body of the citizens and are not to be described. Having girdled the summit with walls, so that none could reach the top nor enter therein, she erected a royal palace, a building of mystery and awe... On the part of the mountain to the east, the surface of which is so hard that even iron can make no mark on it, she caused divers palaces to be hewn from the rock, containing sleeping apartments, treasuries, and long chambers hollowed out of the rock... Over the whole surface of the cliff, as if with a stylus on wax, she carved great numbers of characters. The mere sight of this cliff brings any who behold it into amazement. But this is not the whole tale; for in many places throughout the land of Armenia Queen Samiram erected pillars with similar characters to these, causing various inscriptions to be carved on them."

This account, linked with the name of the Assyrian Queen Sammuramat (812–803 B.C.), attracted particular attention from orientalists when the young archaeologist Friedrich Eduard Schulz, who had been sent to Turkey in 1827 by the French Asiatic Society, reported on the ancient remains he had discovered near the town of Van, on the eastern shores of Lake Van. There was a striking correspondence between Moses Khorenatsi's tale and what Schulz saw at Van. On the high crag which was so circumstantially described by the mediaeval historian were the remains of ancient walls built of huge blocks of stone, with the walls of a later Turkish fortress built on top. Schulz gave a detailed description of the rock-hewn chambers which he found within the fortress, and copied the cuneiform inscriptions which were carved on the cliff, sometimes at the entrances to artificial caves hewn from the rock. He also found large stones from ancient walls with similar inscriptions, and saw a large channel, also ascribed to Queen Samiram, which had brought in water for drinking and irrigation. Near the channel were found other cuneiform inscriptions; and it was only when these were read, half a century later, that the name of the actual constructor of the water channel was revealed. It was the Urartian King Menua (810–781 B.C.), who had been victorious over Queen Sammuramat in real life but had been outshone by her in legend and story.

Schulz's promising work at Van was brought to an untimely end when he was murdered in the mountains near Culamerk. The material which he had sent to Paris in 1828 was not published until 1840. This included accurate copies of 42 cuneiform inscriptions, together with descriptions of the rock-hewn structures of Van and of a number of fortresses.

After Schulz's death no further archaeological work was done at Van for many years. The splendid archaeological discoveries of the 1840s in central Assyria—the excavation of Sargon's palace at Khorsabad and Ashurnasir-pal's at Nimrud—diverted attention to Mesopotamia. A beginning was made with the decipherment of the Assyrian cuneiform, including the in-scriptions from Van; but this work was carried on in isolation, with no asso-ciated archaeological investigation. And when archaeologists showed no interest in Van their place was soon taken by treasure-hunters.

The Museums make their First Acquisitions

Some of the antiquities recovered by clandestine diggers at Van now began to find their way by obscure and devious routes into museums and private collections. Thus the Istanbul Museum acquired two bronze cauldron hand-les representing winged female figures, which were entered in the catalogue as having been found at Van. A few years earlier, in 1859, the Hermitage in St Petersburg had received a similar cauldron handle *(Plates 103–105)*, together with a small representation of a bull's head *(Plate 108)* and some bronze horse trappings (plaques from bridles and bells) *(Plate 76)*. These objects had been recovered from some Kurds, who had found them in an ancient rock-cut tomb on the Russo-Persian frontier, near the frontier post of Alışar. The Keeper of the Hermitage collections, in recording these acquisitions, ascribed them to the culture of Sassanian Iran, since of course he knew nothing of the ancient kingdom of Urartu. He could not foresee that, 95 years later, a cuneiform inscription was to be discovered under the patina on one of the bells, giving the name of the Urartian King Argishti, son of Menua: though even if he had seen the inscription he would have been unable to read it. The Kingdom of Van had sunk into total oblivion, in spite of the references in the Assyrian annals to expeditions into the mountainous areas to the north against various named enemies, including the kings of the land of Urartu.

It was with this forgotten and mysterious country that the inscriptions copied by Schulz, and so made available to scholars, now began to be associated.

In 1871, in Tbilisi (Tiflis), the orientalist M. Brosset published an article on the two winged female figurines from Van in the Istanbul Museum, disagreeing with their attribution to Byzantium and referring them to the culture of Assyria. At the same time he published two letters, one from the great Russian art scholar V.V. Stasov and the other from the eminent French orientalist Prévost de Longpérier. Stasov realised the importance of the figurines, which he believed were to be ascribed neither to the Aryan nor the Semitic culture but reflected a third element in the culture of western Asia— thus foreshadowing the significance of the still unknown Hurrian and Hittite cultures. Longpérier, noting that the closest analogies to the figurines were to be found in Babylonian art, suggested that they might be the work of the Urartians who were mentioned in Assyrian cuneiform inscriptions and were listed by Herodotus, under the name of the Alarodians, among the nations in Xerxes' army.

Thus in the year 1871, with the first correct identification of Urartian works of art, the kingdom of Urartu, which had for so long been utterly forgotten, began at last to emerge from oblivion. In spite of this, however, Urartian objects continued for many years to be regarded as Assyrian and to be displayed in museums along with the rest of the Assyrian material.

Treasure-Hunters and Clandestine Diggers

From the mid-seventies of the 19th century, and still more in the eighties, the quantity of material from Van coming on to the market increased substantially, and the treasure-hunters drove a thriving trade, particularly on the mound of Toprakkale (which was also known to the local inhabitants as Zimzim-Magara).

The work done by R.D. Barnett and myself on the records in London and Leningrad has yielded much interesting information about the channels by which material from Van reached the museums of Europe. One interesting item, for example, is a letter from one of the local inhabitants to Professor Patkanov of St Petersburg University offering to sell certain antiquities which were later acquired by the British Museum. The letter says: "The antiquities in my possession were found near Aygestan in the ruins of the fortress of Zimzim-Magara... In these ruins a great quantity of beautiful things have been found in the past, as for example a large throne, entirely covered with cuneiform inscriptions and gilded; but I am sorry to say that on my return from Europe I learned that it had been broken up and destroyed." Although the signature is indecipherable, Barnett has established beyond any doubt that the writer of the letter must have been Sedrak Devgants, who in the following year offered the objects listed in the letter for sale in Austria. It is a reasonable supposition also that Sedrak Devgants was the "Armenian" in Constantinople who in 1877 sold Henry Layard certain "Assyrian antiquities from Van" for the British Museum, including two figurines from a throne, one of a couchant winged bull, the other of a standing winged bull with forequarters in human form.

Between 1877 and 1885 a number of museums (the British Museum, the Louvre, the Berlin Museum, the Hermitage) and private collections acquired a dozen or so bronze figurines of fantastic animals, covered with gold leaf, decorated with stone inlays, and sometimes with inserted stone heads. Of particular interest is a bronze figurine of a winged lion with forequarters in human form, still retaining traces of its gold coating, and with a face carved from white stone and inlaid eyes of coloured stone, still in an excellent state of preservation *(Plate 101)*. This was bought by the Hermitage in 1882, but letters preserved in the records in London show that it had previously been offered to the British Museum.

These figurines of winged lions and bulls, sometimes with forequarters in human form, and sometimes with gods in human form standing on them, once formed part of the throne referred to in Devgants' letter. The gold and the many-coloured stones with which the throne was decorated must have created an effect of barbaric splendour, and the expressive and terrifying figures of fantastic animals were calculated to inspire superstitious awe in the beholder, as well as to ward off evil influences from the king who occupied the throne. Unfortunately the surviving figurines do not enable us to build up a convincing restoration of the complete throne: it may be, indeed, that they belong not to one throne but to two.

The Beginnings of Archaeology in Central Urartu

The material found by the treasure-hunters gave the stimulus for the first proper archaeological work at Van. In 1877, after his first purchase of Urartian antiquities in Constantinople, Henry Layard sent his assistant Hormuzd Rassam to Van. Rassam had worked closely with Layard in the excavation of the Assyrian palaces, and his name had been associated with many sensational discoveries. At Nineveh he had carried out piratical excavations in the area allotted to the French, had discovered a magnificent room in Ashurbanipal's palace with a representation of a lion hunt, and had located the second part of the famous royal library of clay tablets with cuneiform inscriptions. Later, in the ruins of the palace of Shalmaneser III on the mound of Balawat, he had unearthed the magnificent bronze palace doors, decorated with scenes from Shalmaneser's campaigns, in particular his campaigns against Urartu, with representations of Urartian fortresses, warlike operations, and sacrifices on the shores of Lake Van.

In 1879–80 an expedition from the British Museum worked at Toprakkale under the direction of the British vice-consul in Van, Captain Clayton. Among those who took part in the excavations were Horñuzd Rassam and an American missionary, Dr Raynolds. The site of Toprakkale did not, however, come up to expectations. Although the excavators found the remains of a temple built of carefully dressed blocks of light and dark-coloured stone, fragments of ornamental bronze shields with cuneiform inscriptions and figures of bulls and lions, and a number of smaller pieces, they had looked for more than this. They had hoped to discover monumental buildings like the Assyrian palaces, and were disappointed when these did not appear. Toprakkale seemed to them to be a site of little interest lying on the periphery of Assyrian culture.

Some of the material recovered was displayed in the Assyrian room of the British Museum, but the rest was stored away in crates, and it was not until 80 years later that all this material was examined by R.D. Barnett and properly published. It might seem facetious to say that the material from Toprakkale which the British Museum acquired in 1879–80 only became accessible to scholars when Barnett carried out his further excavations in the storerooms and cellars of the Museum; but perhaps the comment would not be very far from the truth.

In 1898 a German expedition led by C.F. Lehmann-Haupt and W. Belck started work at Toprakkale. By this time the mound had suffered considerably from the attentions of treasure-hunters and the local inhabitants. The whole surface was pitted with trenches, and the stones of the temple discovered by the British expedition had been removed. Lehmann-Haupt cleared the foundations of the temple and drove trenches through different parts of the mound. The excavations brought to light many objects of everyday use, weapons of iron and bronze, implements, pottery and ornaments, and revealed dwelling-houses and store-rooms which had been destroyed by fire; but of Urartian art practically nothing was found. The only items of interest were a bronze candelabrum, the feet of which were decorated with figurines of winged bulls with human heads, a massive foot from a throne, and a thin gold medallion showing a goddess seated on a throne with a woman standing in front of her.

The material obtained by the German expedition also lay in the Berlin Museum for many years, unheeded and unused. It had to wait half a century before it was examined and studied by G.R. Meyer, who discovered many items of great interest, including ornaments which matched those found by the British excavators and a crescent-shaped pendant of electrum representing a goddess seated on a throne. Another item was a bronze candelabrum which was restored in the Hamburg Museum in 1960, when a cuneiform inscription mentioning the name of the Urartian King Rusa was found on the stem.

After the German excavations the Van area was neglected by archaeologists for some years. It was not until the winter of 1911–12 that further exploratory work was carried out on Toprakkale by I.A. Orbeli; then in 1916 the Russian Archaeological Society sent an expedition to Van under the leadership of N.Y. Marr. Marr continued the investigation of Toprakkale, while Orbeli discovered in a niche on the northern face of the crag of Van a large stone stele with a lengthy inscription recording events in the reign of the Urartian King Sarduri II.

Finally, 22 years after the Russian expedition, in the summer of 1938, an American expedition led by K. Lake carried out further work on the crag of Van and on Toprakkale, with the object of checking the dating of the material found by the earlier expeditions. The results achieved by the Americans were of very limited significance, and archaeological work in central Urartu gradually came to a halt, the interest of archaeologists concerned with the ancient East being now concentrated on southern Mesopotamia.

The Exploration of Soviet Armenia

At the same time as interest in the antiquities of central Urartu was dying down, archaeologists were beginning to extend their investigations on the northern borders of the Urartian kingdom, in southern Transcaucasia (now part of the Armenian SSR). For long the only indication that the Ararat valley, the mountainous region round Aragats and the territory round Lake Sevan had belonged to Urartu had been provided by cuneiform inscriptions on rock faces and on stones from ancient buildings. These had been known since 1862, but had been copied and published in an inaccurate form, and had not been associated with any archaeological material. Many stones with cuneiform inscriptions had been found near the mound of Armavir, the site of the ancient capital of Armenia. In 1880 some small-scale excavations were carried out on the mound, but these produced only insignificant results, and the excavators were unable to identify the archaeological level associated with the Urartian cuneiform inscriptions.

In 1893 M. Nikolsky travelled through all the areas in Transcaucasia where cuneiform inscriptions had been found, accompanied by the archaeologist A. Ivanovsky, who made it his business to examine the remains of fortresses in the neighbourhood of the inscriptions. Excavations were carried out at only one place, at the village of Tashburun, on a site which according to the inscriptions had been occupied by the ancient Urartian city of Menuahinili and later became the Armenian town of Tsolakert. The material discovered was mainly mediaeval, which again prevented the excavators from identifying the archaeological level belonging to the Urartian period.

The study of the ancient fortresses situated near the find-spots of Urartian cuneiform inscriptions was resumed in 1930, when there was an upsurge of interest in the remains of antiquity within the territory of the Armenian Soviet Republic. The work then undertaken was in the nature of a reconnaissance, with the object of finding sites justifying more extended excavations.

After a detailed examination of the area which had formed part of the kingdom of Urartu, systematic excavations were begun in 1939 on the mound of Karmir-Blur, on the outskirts of Erevan, where three years before a fragment of stone had been found with the remains of a cuneiform inscription mentioning the name of the Urartian King Rusa, son of Argishti, who reigned in the 7th century B.C.

The excavations at Karmir-Blur, which turned out to be the important Urartian city of Teishebaini, have been carried on for the last 26 years by an expedition under my leadership sponsored jointly by the Armenian Academy of Science and the Hermitage Museum. The citadel, which has been completely excavated, and the districts of the ancient city so far examined have given us a comprehensive picture of the culture and economy of Urartu and of Urartian crafts and building techniques. In the citadel were found a whole series of workshops, store-rooms, wine-cellars and well stocked granaries. In addition to a large quantity of domestic utensils, ornaments, weapons, implements and cloth, stores of grain and the remains of fruit, the excavators found numbers of clay tablets with cuneiform inscriptions—orders from the Urartian king to the governor of this Transcaucasian city and accounting documents dating from the reigns of the last Urartian kings.

The excavations have revealed that Teishebaini superseded earlier Urartian centres in Transcaucasia and that the contents of the store-rooms of these older towns were transferred to the new city. This is shown not only by the occurrence of the names of kings of the 8th century B.C. but also by the place of manufacture of some of the objects found, in particular the bronze shields.

One of these earlier Urartian centres was the city of Erebuni, the name of which is preserved in Erevan, the present capital of Soviet Armenia. The remains of Erebuni were discovered on the mound of Arin-Berd, which lies on the outskirts of Erevan on the opposite side from Karmir-Blur. Excavations were begun here in 1950, at first by a team from the Karmir-Blur expedition and later by an independent expedition organised by the Armenian Academy of Science and the Pushkin Museum in Moscow and led by the architect K. Oganesyan.

The excavations revealed the remains of a palace, two temples, and various store-rooms and domestic offices *(Plates 1–7)*. Some of the rooms had sumptuous painted decorations, including representational pictures as well as purely ornamental patterns *(Plates 8–13)*. Built into the walls of the fortress were twelve foundation inscriptions by two Urartian kings of the 8th century B.C.—Argishti, son of Menua, and Sarduri, son of Argishti— referring to the building of the fortress, the palace, a temple and granaries. The excavations also revealed store-rooms for wine and a hall with many columns which had been reconstructed either during the Urartian period or later. In spite of the excellent state of preservation of the buildings, only a small quantity of material was found in Erebuni. This is understandable, for the town was abandoned during the Urartian period, in the 7th century B.C., and most of the works of art found at Teishebaini seem to have been transferred from Erebuni.

Teishebaini itself was destroyed in the early 6th century B.C. The storming of the fortress was accompanied by a devastating fire, and life never revived in the burnt-out remains. The abandoned fortress of Erebuni was not destroyed but continued to exist into the Achaemenid period; and so the name of the ancient fortress was transferred to the Armenian settlement which grew into a town and is now the capital of Armenia.

Erebuni was mainly an administrative centre, the residence of the Urartian king in Transcaucasia: the centre of the economic life of the area in this period (8th century B.C.) was in the Ararat depression, at Armavir, where the first excavations had produced little result.

In 1964 the Armenian Academy of Science resumed excavation work at Armavir, on the two mounds of Armavir-Blur and David. The directors of excavations were B. Arakelyan and A. Martirosyan. The excavations revealed defensive walls built of large blocks of stone, with the buttresses characteristic of Urartian architecture. On the David mound were discovered the remains of houses belonging to a large town—identified as the Urartian city of Argishtihinili—with cellars containing many implements and utensils of the Urartian period. The mediaeval occupation of the site had played havoc with the Urartian remains, and it is now difficult to determine whether Argishtihinili, like Erebuni, was in a state of decline in the 7th century B.C. The occurrence of similar stamps on jugs found here and at Teishebaini suggests that goods from Argishtihinili as well as from Erebuni were transferred to the store-rooms of the new centre established in the 7th century. Further excavation may be expected to throw more light on this.

Recent Research in Turkey

Recent years have also seen a gradual development of interest in Urartian sites in Turkey. In 1938 the Ankara Museum acquired a collection of material found at Altıntepe, near Erzincan, during the construction of a new railway line. Of particular interest to archaeologists were a bronze tripod cauldron decorated with four bulls' heads, a number of other bronze vessels, a shield, fragments of furniture and other objects; but no further excavation was done on the site for another 21 years—a further example of the slow pace at which the study of Urartian culture has developed.

In 1956–57 the British archaeologist C.A. Burney undertook a survey of the ancient fortresses in the Lake Van area, on the lines of the survey carried out in Armenia between 1930 and 1938. In the course of this he drew plans of many Urartian fortresses associated with previously discovered cuneiform inscriptions. Further inscriptions were published by P. Hulin in *Anatolian Studies*. This work was the prelude to a considerable development of archaeological work in central Urartu. The most extensive excavations in Turkey

1, 2

3, 4

8

9, 10

11

13

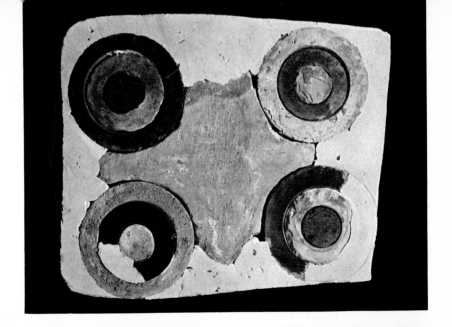

14, 15

were those carried out at Altıntepe by T. Özgüç, which revealed stone-built tombs belonging to persons of high rank, similar in plan to the rock-cut tombs at Van. In these tombs many bronze objects were found—a shield, fittings from furniture, pieces of harness, belts and jewellery. Features of particular interest were a temple similar to the one excavated at Erebuni and a hall with eighteen columns resembling the pillared hall at Erebuni. In the hall were found remains of paintings in many colours and in geometric patterns. The excavations at Altıntepe also yielded pieces of bone carving similar to those found at Toprakkale, decorated with figures of winged demons, palmettes and architectural devices; and they produced a wealth of evidence on Urartian architecture of the 7th century B.C. The tombs were dated by inscriptions of King Rusa and King Argishti.

Between 1959 and 1963 Turkish archaeologists carried out excavations on many different sites. The investigation of the town site of Toprakkale was completed by Afif Erzen, and further work was done on the temple discovered in the earlier excavations by the British Museum. Another bronze shield was found, decorated with figures of lions and bulls and with an inscription in the name of Rusa, son of Erimena. In spite of the disturbed condition of the site the excavators found some still surviving remains of buildings, in particular a wine-cellar containing large storage jars of the type known as *karasy* (the equivalent of the Greek *pithoi*).

Particularly interesting results were obtained at Adılcevaz, on the northern shores of Lake Van, where a large relief of the god Teisheba standing on a bull was found carved on several blocks of stone.

During excavations by E. Bilgiç and B. Öğün in 1964 on the mound of Kefkalesi near Adılcevaz another wine-cellar of the type usual in Urartian fortresses was found, also containing large storage jars marked in cuneiform with an indication of their capacity. In it were found a number of square pillars decorated with carving of remarkable quality—a background of battlemented walls and towers, in front of which were winged demons standing on lions, with sacred trees in front of the towers—together with a badly damaged cuneiform inscription. The archaeologists working here believe that they have located a shrine in the palace of Rusa II, son of Argishti. A cemetery of the Urartian period has also been excavated at Adılcevaz.

An Urartian fortress of the second period (the reign of Sarduri III) was excavated by Erzen on Çavuştepe. The excavations brought to light walls and towers, a temple, domestic buildings of various kinds, and a pottery store. Items of interest found here were fragments of wall paintings and a bronze plaque with representations of chariots and horsemen.

At Patnos Kemal Balkan investigated a number of mounds. On Anzavur-tepe he discovered remains of a temple with inscriptions in the name of Menua and his son Argishti I; and our knowledge of Urartian art was extended by the finding of a figurine of a lion, a gold necklace with small pendants, bracelets and seals.

In 1955 excavations were begun on the mound of Kayalidere in the vilayet of Muş by the Institute of Archaeology of the University of London (Seton Lloyd, C.A. Burney). The first excavation season was successful, with the discovery of remains of a fortress, a wine-store and a temple. The small finds included a bronze figurine of a lion which had decorated one of the feet of a candelabrum, fragments of a belt decorated with a scene representing a lion-hunt from a chariot, ornamental elements from furniture, and iron weapons.

Progress and Prospects

Thus we see that the archaeological study of Urartian culture has travelled a long and arduous road; a road full of difficulties and disappointments, with many periods of delay and stagnation. The archaeologists working in the area round Lake Van in the 19th century were for the most part merely following in the footsteps of the treasure-hunters: the only proper excavations were those on Toprakkale, and even here there were long intervals when no progress was made.

The investigation of Urartian sites in Transcaucasia which began 35 years ago has substantially enlarged our knowledge of Urartu; much evidence has been accumulated on the economy, the culture, and the art of the Urartians; and their cultural links with other countries of the ancient East have been established. As a result it has become possible to produce general studies of Urartian history and culture. Collections of Urartian cuneiform inscriptions have been compiled (G. Melikishvili, F.W. König), the evidence from Assyrian and Babylonian sources has been brought together (I. Dyakonov), the study of the language of the Vannic cuneiform inscriptions has made substantial progress (J. Friedrich, A. Goetze, I. Meshchaninov, G. Melikishvili, I. Dyakonov, N. Arutyunyan), the Urartian material from the older excavations has been reviewed (R. D. Barnett, G.R. Meyer), and the first study of Urartian art has been produced (E. Akurgal).

The last ten years have seen a remarkable development of interest in the ancient kingdom of Urartu. Excavations in the Armenian SSR are continuing with considerable success, and archaeological investigations in Turkey, in the central part of the Urartian kingdom, are in process of intensive development, striving to make up for the neglect of earlier years. At international congresses of orientalists increasing interest is being shown in the culture of the Kingdom of Van, and a number of studies have been produced dealing with its relationships with the Scythian world, the Caucasus, Asia Minor and the Mediterranean. Particular attention is being paid to the links between Urartian art and the art of archaic Greece and the Etruscans (Massimo Pallottino). The cultural heritage of Urartu is now seen to be considerably more extensive than had been supposed.

There can be no doubt that archaeologists are standing on the threshold of important new discoveries which will give still further impetus to the study of this ancient kingdom after so many centuries of neglect.

THE PROBLEM OF ORIGINS

Early Cultures in Armenia

Although the written sources and the archaeological evidence available to us are still insufficient to give a clear picture of the formation of the Urartian kingdom and its early history, we do know that the kingdom of Urartu grew out of the fusion of related Hurrian tribes living in the Armenian highlands, particularly in the region round Lake Van, where conditions were especially favourable for the development of the two associated activities of stock-rearing and agriculture.

The mountains of Kurdistan, lying to the south of the Armenian highlands, are one of the most considerable ranges in western Asia, constituting a formidable barrier to human movement with their forbidding crags and their densely wooded slopes. In the 3rd and 2nd millennia B.C. these mountains separated two regions of western Asia with quite distinct cultures—the mountain area and the lowland area. To the south of the mountains was the advanced agricultural culture of Mesopotamia and the plain areas, known from many archaeological sites and producing a characteristic type of painted pottery decorated with designs reflecting the symbolism of agricultural and stock-rearing cults.

To the north of the mountains of Kurdistan, however, was a very different culture which produced no painted pottery, but used instead a highly polished black ware decorated with moulded or incised ornament. The development of productive forces proceeded less vigorously in the mountain regions and the Armenian upland plateau than in the south: a fact which explains the slower pace of social and political development among the highland tribes.

The most recent archaeological investigations show that in the 3rd millennium B.C. a uniform pattern of culture extended over the southern Caucasus area north of the River Araxes, the area round Lake Van, eastern Anatolia and the region round Lake Urmia. The basis of the economy of this culture was a combination of primitive forms of agriculture and stock-rearing, particular stress being laid on stock-rearing, which more readily yielded a surplus product at a relatively rudimentary stage of development of productive forces. As a result the culture which had originally developed in the river valleys and at the outfalls of mountain streams began in the second half of the 3rd millennium B.C. to spread to the foothill areas, thus creating a cultural unity over a considerable territory. This had connections with the Hurrian civilisation, the western part of the Armenian highlands, the basin of the River Habur, and northern Syria; and links can also be traced with the southern Caucasus. Thus in the *kurgans* (burial mounds) of the 17th and 16th centuries B.C. excavation has revealed fine chased gold and silver cups and bronze weapons (Trialeti, Kirovakan), providing evidence of connections with Asia Minor and Syria.

In *kurgans* of the following period which were excavated at the village of Lchashen, on the western shore of Lake Sevan, and in a cemetery at the village of Artik on the slopes of Mount Aragats were found Mitannian cylinder seals dating from the end of the 15th or the beginning of the 14th century B.C.—i.e., from the final phase of the Mitannian kingdom. These finds are clear evidence of ancient cultural links.

After the destruction of Mitanni by the Hittites at the turn of the 15th and 14th centuries B.C. the Armenian highland areas maintained their links with the Hittites, which had now begun to expand into northern Syria. These relationships with other nations played an important part in the development of the culture of the highland areas; and by the time the Hittite kingdom fell, about the year 1200 B.C., the tribes of the Armenian highlands had achieved a relatively high level of cultural and social development. They were now able to form powerful alliances of tribes and challenge the northward advance of the Assyrians, who after the fall of Mitanni had entered on a period of political expansion.

Uruatri and Nairi in the Second Millennium B.C.

And it is in fact from Assyrian documents of the 13th century B.C. that we gain our first definite information about the peoples of the Armenian highlands. In inscriptions of the Assyrian King Shalmaneser I (1280–1261 B.C.) we find the first occurrence of the term Uruatri, applied to a group of countries against which the Assyrian king mounted a campaign in the early years of his reign. The inscriptions record the conquest of eight countries, collectively referred to as Uruatri, situated in a mountainous region to the south-east of Lake Van—perhaps in the upper valley of the Greater Zab. It must be borne in mind that the Assyrians' quarrel was with the peoples on their frontiers, and we do not know how far the territory occupied by the Uruatri tribes actually extended. It is very likely that the tribes living in the area round Lake Van were also included in the alliance; for the Assyrian name of Uruatri had no ethnic significance but was most probably a descriptive term (perhaps meaning "the mountainous country").

In texts written in the name of the Assyrian King Tukulti-Ninurta I, son of Shalmaneser I, we find another collective designation for the alliance of the tribes of the Armenian highlands. They are now known as "the lands of Nairi": a term which for almost a century replaced the name of Uruatri (Urartu). Inscriptions found in the palace and temple of Tukulti-Ninurta in Assur tell how 43 kings of the lands of Nairi rose up against Assyria, how they were defeated, and how the kings of Nairi were brought in chains to Assur. Then the lands of Nairi offered valuable gifts to the king of Assyria, tribute was exacted from them, and a new honour was added to the official style of the Assyrian king—"king of all the lands of Nairi".

A detailed account of the Assyrian expedition to the north, into the lands of Nairi, from the sources of the Tigris to the land of Daiani, in the basin of the River Chorokh (Çoruh), is preserved in the annals of Tiglath-Pileser I (1116–1090 B.C.). The campaign was directed not against the region to the south-east of Lake Van, as Shalmaneser I's expedition had been, but against the whole of the western part of the Armenian highland area, from north to south. In the course of the campaign the Assyrians penetrated into enemy territory to a depth of more than 300 miles.

The Assyrian annals describe the campaign in the following words: "The god Ashur, my lord and master, sent me against the lands of the distant kings who dwell on the shore of the Upper Sea (i.e., the Black Sea), owning no master; and thither I went. By toilsome paths and arduous passes, through which no king before me had gone, by hidden tracks and unmade roads I led my armies... Where the going was easy I travelled in my chariot; where it was difficult I advanced with the help of brazen axes (i.e., clearing a path)... Twenty-three kings of the lands of Nairi gathered together chariots and warriors in their countries and rose up against me in war and strife. I advanced against them with all the fury of my dread armament and, like Adad's flood, annihilated their great army... Sixty kings of the lands of Nairi, together with those who came to their aid, did I drive with my spear as far as the Upper Sea. I captured their great cities, I carried off their riches and their spoils, I gave their dwellings to the flames... All the kings of the lands of Nairi did I capture alive. But to all these kings I showed mercy, granting them their lives in the sight of Shamash, my lord and master, and freeing them from the bonds of captivity. Then I caused them to swear on oath to my great gods that they would serve me and obey me in all time to come; and their sons, the heirs to their royal houses, I took as hostages to their word. Then I exacted tribute from them, twelve hundred horses and two thousand head of cattle, and let them return to their own countries...".

The inscriptions thus give us a brief but vivid account of the Assyrian expedition into the western Armenian highlands at the end of the 12th century B.C. The Assyrian king's aim was not merely to defeat and plunder these wealthy countries: by his merciful treatment of the captured kings he sought to strengthen his authority in the Lands of Nairi. It is also to be noted that in the account of the campaign there is no mention of the area round Lake

Van (the "Sea of Nairi"). It may be that the Assyrians deliberately avoided the central part of the area occupied by the powerful league of enemy tribes, where they might have encountered stronger resistance.

In Assyrian inscriptions of the 11th century B.C. we again find the term Uruatri, and from the second quarter of the 9th century, in the reign of Ashurnasirpal II (883–859 B.C.), it is of common occurrence, in the form Urartu, being used concurrently with the name of Nairi—and at first without any clear demarcation between the two.

The Campaigns of Shalmaneser III and the Balawat Gates

In the history of western Asia the middle of the 9th century is marked by an intensification of warlike activity by Assyria, which had now re-established its military strength. Assyrian control of the territories it conquered was achieved by fire and sword, and the war against its enemies who remained unsubdued was waged with extraordinary ruthlessness. Nevertheless resistance increased in the countries against which the Assyrian campaigns were directed; the smaller tribes came together in larger alliances, and new states gradually developed out of these groupings. In this way the state of Urartu came into being in the first half of the 9th century B.C.; and by this time the name had already begun to take on an ethnic connotation.

From the beginning of his reign, therefore, the Assyrian King Shalmaneser III (860–825 B.C.) found himself at war with this new enemy—which, however, had not yet developed into a centralised state. We are well informed about Shalmaneser's campaigns against Urartu not only from the annals, which give detailed accounts of the route followed by the Assyrian army and of its victories, but also from the representations of episodes from the expedition on the bronze gates which were found in 1878 in the ruins of the ancient city of Imgur-Enlil on the mound of Balawat, south-east of Nineveh.

On one of the gates, which are outstanding examples of Assyrian art, are represented episodes from a campaign in the first year of Shalmaneser's reign (860 B.C.) which is very briefly described in his annals in these words: "I drew near to Sugunia, the stronghold of Aramu the Urartian; I invested the town and captured it; I killed many of their warriors and carried off plunder; I made a pile of heads over against their city; fourteen settlements in its territory I gave to the flames. Then I departed from Sugunia and went down to the Sea of Nairi, where I washed my weapons in the sea and offered a sacrifice to my gods."

The gates give a pictorial narrative of a connected series of events which took place at different times and places. The scenes are contained in two bands or registers, telling a consecutive story which begins in the bottom left-hand corner with a picture of the Assyrian army's camp. The army, consisting of chariots and infantry, is shown marching out of the camp against Sugunia, the Urartian fortress mentioned in the annals. There is also a representation of the capture of Sugunia, showing a fortress situated on a hill, in flames, which is being stormed on both sides with the aid of ladders laid up against the walls. Inside the fortress can be seen the defenders—Urartian warriors, both spearmen and archers. Above the whole scene is the explanatory legend: "I vanquished Sugunia, the city of Aramu the Urartian." To the right of this scene is a group of Urartian prisoners. The upper band shows the march of the Assyrian army over three passes to Lake Van, and in the top left-hand corner is a representation of Shalmaneser's sacrifice on the shores of the lake and the setting up of a stele with a figure of the Assyrian king. The sacrifice is offered by the king in person; beside him stand two priests, and in the background are musicians and sacrificial animals. Above this scene is the legend: "This statue, my own image, I set up by the sea of the Land of Nairi; I offered a sacrifice to my gods."

In other scenes are represented episodes from Shalmaneser's later campaigns, in particular the capture of Arzashku, the royal city—though not the capital—of "Aramu the Urartian", which was achieved during an expedition in the third year of Shalmaneser's reign. This was a lengthy expedition following a very similar route to that of Tiglath-Pileser I. The Assyrians approached Arzashku through the land of Daiani, and their annals tell the story in these words: "Aramu the Urartian, being struck with fear by the terror of my mighty army and my mighty battle, withdrew from his city"— and the gates give us a picture of the burning fortress, abandoned by its defenders—"and went up into the mountains of Adduri. Then I went up after him and fought a mighty battle in the mountains. With my arms I overthrew 3,400 warriors; like Adad, I brought a great rain-cloud down upon them; with the blood of the enemy I dyed the mountain as if it had been wool; and I captured their camp... Then Aramu, to save his life, fled to an inaccessible mountain. In my mighty strength I trampled on his land like a wild bull; and his cities I reduced to ruins and consumed with fire." In a later passage the annals record the ascent of Mount Eritna, where a large stele was erected with a figure of the Assyrian king, and an expedition to the land of Armali and from there to Lake Van, where the Assyrians washed their weapons in the lake, offered sacrifices and again set up a stele with a likeness of the king.

The Balawat gates depict the burning fortress of Arzashku, with a double line of walls. Outside the fortress we see a battle between Assyrians and Urartians, with the latter withdrawing to the mountains. An episode from the same campaign may be represented in a scene on the gates which bears the brief legend "A battle against Urartu". This again shows a fight between Assyrians and Urartians and a large burning fortress, with Assyrians felling trees and laying waste the countryside. A later scene shows a small fortress with the defeated enemy impaled on stakes and a pile of heads under the walls. A four-wheeled vehicle drawn by men is shown leaving the fortress laden with booty contained in a large *karas*. Vessels of this kind, which have been found in the excavations of Urartian fortresses, were primarily intended for the storage of wine, but were also used for the safe keeping of valuables and foodstuffs during a siege.

The Urartian Kingdom in the 9th Century B.C.

The bronze gates of Balawat are of great interest for the light they throw on the culture of Urartu, since they give the earliest known representations of the Urartians, with exact delineations of their clothing and weapons. They are shown wearing short-sleeved tunics reaching to their knees, gathered at the waist by a broad belt, probably of bronze. On their heads are helmets of characteristic type with low crests. They are armed with bows, spears and small round shields with a central boss.

In clothing and equipment the Urartians differed from the Assyrians and showed closer affinities with the Hurrians and Hittites. An example of this is the crested helmet, which came into use in Assyria only in the mid-8th century B.C., having been taken over from the Urartians.

On the evidence of Shalmaneser III's annals the Urartian kingdom already occupied a considerable territory, for the Assyrian king is recorded as waging war against the Urartians and destroying the fortresses of Aramu the Urartian in a number of different areas in the Armenian highlands. The events of the campaigns of the first and third years of Shalmaneser's reign are described in detail, but the events of later years, and in particular of the fifteenth year of his reign, are only very briefly recorded. The annals give a laconic account of the Assyrians' arduous march through the mountains, but there is no mention of any expeditions into central Urartu, the region round Lake Van. This can be seen as an indication of the growing power of Urartu: no doubt Shalmaneser was well aware of the danger looming up in the north, but had inadequate resources to avert it.

At the end of Shalmaneser's reign the Assyrians had once again to send a force against Urartu; but in the 27th year of his reign the aged king was no longer able to take command himself, and the army which he sent "against the land of Urartu" was led by his general Daian-Ashur. When the Assyrians crossed the River Arzani (Aratsani), "Siduri (Sarduri), ruler of Urartu, heard of this and, being confident in the strength of his great army, pressed forward to join battle." Thus twelve years after the last mention of the Urartian ruler Aramu in the annals of the year 834 B.C. we encounter a new ruler bearing the name of Siduri (Sarduri), which henceforth is of frequent occurrence in the dynasty of the kings of Urartu.

From the third quarter of the 9th century, too, date the oldest known Urartian sites, in the area of Lake Van.

At the foot of the western side of the crag of Van, the citadel of the Urartian capital of Tushpa, are the remains of a massive cyclopean wall built of colossal blocks of stone 2½ feet thick and up to 20 feet long, which may have been a pier or breakwater stretching out into the lake. On the wall are three inscriptions in Assyrian, all with the same purport, in the name of Sarduri, the king mentioned in the Assyrian annals of the year 834 B.C. The text of the inscriptions is as follows: "An inscription of Sarduri, son of Lutipri, the magnificent king, the mighty king, king of the universe, king of the land of Nairi, a king having none equal to him, a shepherd to be wondered at, fearing no battle, a king who humbled those who would not submit to his authority. I, Sarduri, son of Lutipri, king of kings, received tribute from all the kings. Sarduri, son of Lutipri, says: 'I procured this limestone from the city of Alniunu, I erected this wall.'"

Historians have been unable to determine whether the "Sarduri, son of Lutipri" mentioned in the inscription was a descendant of Aramu or whether he belonged to another dynasty. The available evidence does not enable us to answer this question, nor to suggest any other site as the original capital of Urartu; but in the twelve years between the occurrence of the name of Aramu and the later reference to Sarduri there is clearly room for another intervening king.

The region round Lake Van enjoyed a favourable geographical and strategic situation, and it was quite natural that it should be chosen as the centre of a politically unified state from the earliest times. It is more difficult to suppose that such a centre would be situated in an inaccessible mountain area with limited scope for the development of agriculture and communications with other parts of the Armenian highlands.

The Rise of Urartu

The inscription by Sarduri I is written in Assyrian—indicating that the nascent Urartian state had already assimilated certain elements of the culture of its enemy, Assyria, including in particular the art of writing. The less advanced hieroglyphic script remained in use only for administrative and accounting purposes. It is noteworthy also that the Urartian king refers to himself in the inscription as "king of the land of Nairi", using the old Assyrian style.

We have also an inscription by King Ishpuini, son of Sarduri I—the Kelishin Stele—which is written in both languages, Assyrian and Urartian. The title "king of the land of Nairi" in the Assyrian text is matched by the title "king of the land of Biaini" in the Urartian one. The latter term, "land of Biaini", was the one usually applied by the Urartians to their country in the following period, from the end of the 9th century onwards. The term, a collective plural form, later came to be used in two different senses—as the name of the central part of the kingdom (i.e., the area round Lake Van), and as a general term for the country as a whole, as distinct from the hostile territory which surrounded it. But since the term Urartu was widely used in the ancient

East as a name for the Kingdom of Van, it tended to displace the phonetically accurate term Biaini(li) which the Urartians applied to themselves.

The evidence reviewed in this chapter shows that the Urartians first appear in history in the 13th century B.C. as a league of tribes or countries which did not yet constitute a unitary state. In the Assyrian annals the term Uruatri (Urartu) as a name for this league was superseded during a considerable period of years by the term "land of Nairi"—a designation which also comprehended the region round Lake Van, the lake itself being known as the "Sea of Nairi". In the 9th century B.C. the Assyrians advancing northward already encountered strong resistance from the Urartians, led by their rulers Aramu and Siduri. The "land of Urartu" had now developed into a kingdom which continued—with varying fortunes—to wage a stubborn fight against its enemy. By the end of the 9th century the power of Urartu had increased to such an extent that Assyria was compelled to recognise its dominance in western Asia. From this period began the political and cultural rise of Urartu, which made it for two centuries the largest state in western Asia, occupying the whole of the Armenian highland area.

23, 24

25, 26

29

30

31

32

HISTORY AND ARCHAEOLOGY

The First Great Reigns

The earliest surviving inscriptions in the Urartian language date from the reign of King Ishpuini, son of Sarduri, who is mentioned in the Assyrian annals of the year 824 B.C. The primitive hieroglyphic script proved inadequate to the needs of the rapidly rising Urartian kingdom, and accordingly the Urartians took over the Assyrian cuneiform script at the end of the 9th century B.C., altering and simplifying the form of the characters in some respects and adapting the script to their own language. The local hieroglyphic script retained a restricted role for accounting and cult purposes.

On the evidence of the inscriptions the reign of Ishpuini, son of Sarduri, was marked by the erection of many temples, fortresses and other buildings both in the capital city of Tushpa and in the surrounding area. Of all these buildings, however, only fragmentary remains have survived: in many cases nothing is left but a few stones with cuneiform inscriptions.

The reign of King Menua (Minua), son of Ishpuini, saw the beginning of the ascendancy of Urartu. In the wars with Assyria the advantage now began to pass to Urartu; but in spite of their contiguity there were no direct clashes between the two countries, separated as they were by an almost impenetrable range of high, densely forested mountains.

In many parts of his kingdom Menua constructed towns, fortresses, palaces and temples, laid out water channels, and planted gardens and vineyards. All these activities, along with the victories won by his armies, are recorded in numerous cuneiform inscriptions.

Menua pursued a vigorous programme of building in the capital, Tushpa, erecting massive walls round the citadel on the crag, extending the town which lay on the shores of the salt lake, bringing in drinking water by means of an aqueduct driven through more than 50 miles of rugged country. At certain points the channel was carried on walls built of huge blocks of stone, and at such places there were always memorial inscriptions recording the name of the builder and cursing any who should destroy the structure or claim the credit for building it.

The extension of Urartian territory was accompanied by a strengthening of central authority, the emergence of a ruling class, the creation of a system of administration of the various regions, and the establishment of a pantheon of gods which accommodated a large number of minor divinities previously worshipped by the various separate tribes. The pantheon was headed by the triad of gods worshipped in central Urartu—Haldi, Teisheba and Shivini.

In a niche in the mountains near Van, now known as Mheri-Dur ("the Gate of Mhera"), there has been preserved a long text of the end of the 9th century B.C., inscribed in duplicate, listing a total of 79 gods and prescribing the sacrifices (of bulls, cows and sheep) which were due to them.

The most important Urartian god, and the one to whom most inscriptions are dedicated, was Haldi. This supreme god of the Urartian pantheon was represented in the form of a man (sometimes bearded, sometimes beardless, like all the other gods) standing on a lion *(Plate 13)*. He had as his wife the goddess Arubani. Haldi was a warrior god who blessed the king when he set out on a campaign, to whom the king prayed for victory, to whom an account was given of all military successes. In the temples dedicated to Haldi there is clear evidence of a cult of weapons: swords, spears, bows and arrows were laid up in the temples, their walls were hung with shields, and the temple itself was sometimes known as the "house of weapons".

The second place in the Urartian pantheon was occupied by Teisheba, the god of storms and thunder, who was designated by the Assyrian ideogram for the god Adad. He was homonymous with the Hurrian god Teshub, who was widely worshipped in Asia Minor, and was represented in the form of a man standing on a bull, often holding a handful of thunderbolts. His wife was Huba, corresponding to the Hurrian goddess Hebat.

The third god in the pantheon was the sun god Shivini, whose name was often written with the Assyrian ideogram for Shamash. He was represented in the form of a kneeling man holding up the winged solar disc which was his symbol. Shivini's wife was probably the goddess Tushpuea, who occupies third place in the list of goddesses in the Mheri-Dur inscription. The winged female figures often found as ornaments on the cauldrons used for cult purposes may represent this goddess.

The Urartian pantheon also included the gods of the conquered cities and territories, and gods associated with totemistic and animistic beliefs. Thus, for example, the list includes "the god of the town of Arda (i.e., Musasir)", "the god of the town of Kumanu", "the god of the town of Tushpa (the capital of the kingdom)", and "the god of the town of Haldi". These were the gods of the various cities, each an important religious centre, which formed part of the Urartian kingdom.

Among the divinities reflecting totemistic conceptions we find gods of the earth, the sea, water, mountains, caves, and so on.

We can see, therefore, that the religion of Urartu reflected cultural and political elements which bound together large territories in western Asia, combining them with ancient local beliefs.

Of particular interest in this connection is one of the oldest Urartian temples, which according to the written sources was built by the Urartians in the city of Musasir at the end of the 9th century B.C., and is depicted in a relief in the palace of the Assyrian King Sargon showing the sacking of Musasir in the year 714 B.C. The temple, built on a high platform, has a pitched roof with a high pediment, on top of which is a device in the form of a spear. The façade has six columns, with a low door in the centre. The walls and columns are decorated with metal (gold and silver) shields, and at the entrance are two bronze statues in an attitude of prayer and two large spears.

It is clear at the first glance that the Urartian temple depicted in Sargon's relief is quite different from the temples of Mesopotamia, being more akin to the temples of Asia Minor which became the prototypes for the classical Greek temples. A similar link can be seen in the winged female figures, similar to those on the Urartian cauldrons, which are found in archaic Greek temples and in Etruscan tombs. Many of these are Urartian; others have been copied from Urartian models but show distinctive stylistic features of their own.

Unfortunately, although we have a large number of inscriptions in the name of King Menua, the architecture and art of his reign are much more poorly represented—a deficiency which is likely to be made good by further archaeological work in the territory of Urartu.

The expansion of Urartu continued in the reign of Argishti, son of Menua, who succeeded to the throne in the first quarter of the 8th century B.C.

In the citadel of Van, beside a large chamber hewn from the rock which may have been the king's tomb, is a long cuneiform inscription known as the "Chronicle of Horhor". It tells of numerous campaigns which extended the frontiers of Urartu, of the annexation of new territories, and of the king's building operations. At the very outset of his reign Argishti embarked on expeditions to the west, seeking to achieve an outlet to the Mediterranean and to capture the main trade routes controlled by the Assyrians. Argishti's war with Assyria is also described in inscriptions by the Assyrian governor Shamshi-ilu, who kept open the route to the sea, in his palace at Til-Barsip on the Euphrates.

At the same time as he undertook these campaigns in the west Argishti conquered and annexed territory in Transcaucasia north of the Araxes valley.

Erebuni and Argishtihinili

In the fourth year of the "Chronicle of Horhor" there are references to expeditions into northern Syria against the countries of Hatti and Melita, and in the following year there is an account of further conquests in the north and of the building of the city of Erebuni "to declare the might of the land of Biaini and hold her enemies in awe". It is particularly recorded that 6,600 prisoners captured in the lands of Hatti and Tsupani (i.e., in the campaigns of the previous year) were settled in the new town. The transfer of prisoners over considerable distances was a regular practice of rulers in the ancient East, serving the double purpose of weakening the enemy and providing a large labour force. In this case the prisoners had to traverse something like 450 miles of difficult country, and were thus completely cut off from their homeland.

The city of Erebuni was established in the foothill area on the edge of the Araxes valley and served as a base for the Urartian advance into the area round Lake Sevan, a mountainous region, rich in cattle, occupied by tribes with a culture of Hurrian pattern. The citadel of Erebuni, containing a royal palace, a temple and store-rooms, was built on the elongated hill of Arin-Berd and was approximately triangular in plan *(Plates 1–7)*. Systematic excavations began in 1959, and fifteen years' work by the archaeologists has made it possible to build up a complete picture of the citadel. Coming through the entrance gates, the visitor would find himself in a wide courtyard (later built up), with the temple complex on the left, store-rooms on the right, and the façade of the temple in front of him. Into the walls were built inscriptions indicating the function of the buildings and the names of the builders (Argishti I and his son Sarduri II). The main temple was a long building decorated with wall paintings, of which some decorative friezes and a figure of the god Haldi on a lion have survived *(Plate 13)*. Along the front was a colonnade with two rows of columns, and to the left was a tower. The palace was a complex of buildings serving a variety of different purposes. A flight of steps led up into an open peristyle courtyard (i.e., with columns round the perimeter), on the west side of which was a small *"susi"* temple *(Plate 6)*, consisting of a single rectangular chamber with inscriptions on either side of the entrance indicating that it was built by Argishti I and dedicated to the god Iubsha (Iuarsha). On the east side were various state apartments, including a room richly decorated with paintings of Assyrian type consisting of bands of ornament in geometric patterns and representations of a sacred tree with genii standing on either side of it and large figures of bulls and lions *(Plates 8–12)*. The main colours used are white (for the background), black (for outlining the drawing), red and blue (for filling in the pattern). The closest analogies to these paintings are found in the Assyrian palaces, particularly Ashurnasirpal's palace in Kalhu (Nimrud).

To the north of the courtyard were various buildings, including rooms with central columns and store-rooms for wine and other produce. In the wine-cellars were large earthenware jars, some of them with a capacity of more than 200 gallons, sunk into the earth floor. On the north side of the palace was another open courtyard surrounded by a number of small rooms.

The eastern part of the citadel was occupied by a large building with a pillared central chamber for the storage of wine. This was surrounded by small store-rooms, some of them used as granaries. The central chamber was richly decorated with paintings, sometimes representational (hunting scenes, the driving of cattle, sacrifices), sometimes purely ornamental. The excavation of this room is still in progress, and is yielding some outstanding examples of Urartian decorative art.

At some time in the life of Erebuni—perhaps in the Urartian period, perhaps later—the buildings in the citadel were reconstructed, and the colonnade in front of the main temple was extended and enclosed by a wall, producing a square hall with thirty columns like an Achaemenid *apadana* screening the entrance to the palace. The central chamber of the store-room block was also altered: in this building column bases with inscriptions by Argishti I and broken wine-jars *(pithoi)* were found under the new floor.

The excavators of Erebuni also discovered a large complex of well-preserved buildings constructed of adobe brick on a stone plinth. These contained fragments of wall paintings, which give some idea of the sumptuous decoration of the rooms and constitute a small museum of Urartian decorative art, but only a negligible quantity of the artefacts usually found in excavations. This suggests that in the 8th century B.C. the fortress of Erebuni was a place of bustling activity, the residence of the Urartian king who was in personal command of the campaigns which added new territories to his kingdom, with ambassadors constantly arriving at the fortress and tribute being delivered to the store-rooms, but that later the fortress was abandoned, the treasures heaped up in its store-rooms were transferred elsewhere, and only the merest flicker of life was left in Erebuni. This no doubt explains why the excavators found only a few small objects preserved by chance—seals, ornaments, and articles of bronze and iron—and fragments of pottery which made it possible to establish the types of vessels produced by Urartian potters.

Erebuni was an important military and administrative centre, maintaining the Urartian king's authority over the newly conquered territories and providing a base for further military operations. But in order to develop the resources of the rich Ararat depression in the valley of the River Araxes—considered one of the most fertile regions in the whole of western Asia—it was essential to establish a new centre of economic life in the area. The metal in the conquered regions had been carried off, and the slaves and cattle driven to other areas; and it was therefore necessary to develop farming and horticulture in place of metalworking and stock-rearing. We know from numerous inscriptions that the Urartians carried out large-scale works for the improvement of the Araxes valley: channels were constructed to draw water from the river, gardens and vineyards were planted on the irrigated land, and large areas were laid out in fields.

Six years after the foundation of Erebuni, therefore, Argishti established a new city as a centre of economic life in the valley of the Araxes, calling it Argishtihinili ("built by Argishti"). The town itself occupied a large area on a long ridge of hills, and round it, in the level country below, was a great belt of fields, gardens and vineyards. The city was encircled by strong defensive works—massive stone walls reinforced by towers—within which were farmsteads, temples and store-rooms. Inside the citadel was a palace.

Large numbers of inscriptions, mainly foundation and cult inscriptions, bear witness to the importance of Argishtihinili; and the excavations in progress here have confirmed the evidence of the inscriptions. Some well-preserved houses have been excavated, with various domestic utensils and equipment in the cellars, sections of the walls have been cleared, a new foundation inscription has been found, a temple which continued in use into the mediaeval period has been discovered, and many characteristic Urartian objects have been recovered. The subsequent destiny of Argishtihinili has not yet, however, been established: we do not know whether it continued in full activity after the fall of Erebuni, or whether this centre of 8th century economic life was superseded by new centres elsewhere.

Urartu and Assyria in the 8th Century B.C.

By the end of Argishti I's reign, in the middle of the 8th century B.C., Urartu was at the zenith of its power. Its authority was firmly established in the north, in Transcaucasia, and in the region round Lake Urmia. It had successfully advanced into Hittite territory in the west. Northern Syria was

34

39. 40

42

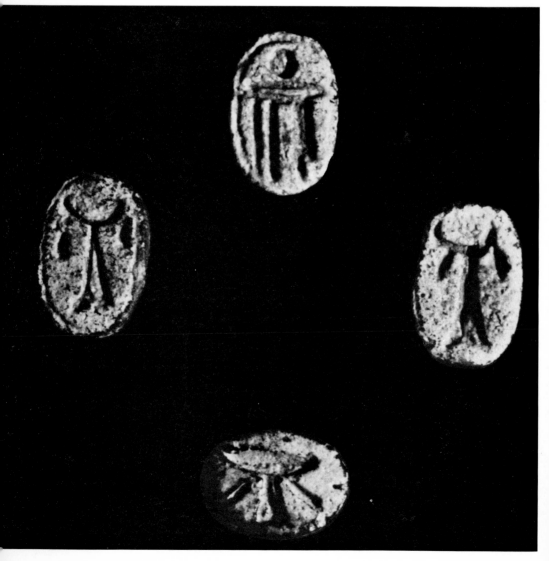

45

dependent on Urartu, which now controlled the main trade routes of western Asia. The Urartian kingdom barred the way to the conquest of Asia Minor by the Assyrians, and Urartian culture had begun to penetrate into the Mediterranean area and the interior of Asia Minor. Urartian objects—small jars in the form of animals' heads and large bronze cauldrons decorated with bulls' heads and winged figures—have been found in the tomb of a Phrygian king at Gordion (middle of 8th century B.C.); and, as we have already noted, similar examples of Urartian work penetrated not only into insular and mainland Greece but as far afield as Italy.

The rise of Urartu and its seizure of the route to the Mediterranean vitally affected the interests of Assyria and relegated it to a secondary position; but Assyria was in a temporary economic and political retrogression and unable to resist the advance of Urartu, and one area after another fell away from its allegiance.

The Urartian army had now developed into a formidable striking force. In this as in other fields, however, the Urartians owed a great deal to their enemies the Assyrians. In the 9th century B.C. Urartian military equipment had been similar to that of the Hurrian tribes and quite different from that of the Assyrians; but by the reign of Argishti, as we know both from representations of arms and armour in works of art and from actual examples found by excavation, Assyrian equipment (helmets, shields, clothing and weapons) had become the regular wear of the Urartian army. Similarly the culture and the way of life of the ruling class of the Kingdom of Van were deeply imbued with Assyrian influence. This is clearly evident in the surviving examples of court art.

On succeeding to the throne in the middle of the 8th century B.C. Sarduri, son of Argishti, inherited a prosperous and flourishing kingdom. He maintained his father's external policy, pursued a vigorous building programme in the central part of the kingdom, and continued to strengthen and develop the existing administrative and economic centres—as is shown by the fact that inscriptions by Argishti I and Sarduri II are usually found in close proximity to one another.

The crag of Van still remained the citadel of the capital, Tushpa, and in two large niches on its southern slope Sarduri set up two stelae recording the annals of his reign. Unfortunately only one of these, with the lower part damaged, has survived, recounting the events of nine years of the king's reign. Of the second stele, which recorded Sarduri's successful wars against Assyria, only fragments remain. This second stele contained information about the land of Arme, in the upper Tigris valley, which after the collapse of Urartu became the nucleus of a new tribal association of Armenians, the ancestors of the present-day Armenian people. The complete annals seem to have covered a period of 22 years. They make it evident that in the reign of Sarduri II the territory of Urartu continued to extend and its power to grow. The Euphrates became the strongly defended western frontier of the kingdom, and Urartian authority was still powerfully asserted in the regions to the north of the Araxes and round Lake Urmia.

Inscriptions by Sarduri II referring to his new building operations have been found in Erebuni. The tribes living on the shores of Lake Sevan were being finally subdued, and new fortresses were being built in this area. Argishti-hinili continued to prosper, and Sarduri devoted much attention to its development.

The tranquillity of Sarduri's reign, however, was interrupted by the revival of Assyria. In the year 745 B.C., after a rising in Kalhu and the accession to the Assyrian throne of Tiglath-Pileser III, the situation in western Asia underwent a radical change. The new Assyrian king carried out a reorganisation of the army which considerably increased its effectiveness, and was then able to set about re-establishing the former frontiers of his kingdom and recovering the territories it had lost.

Assyria was of course particularly disturbed by the establishment of Urartian authority in northern Syria, and as early as the third year of his reign (743 B.C.) Tiglath-Pileser moved westward and in a battle at Arpad defeated the army of the Urartians, who were allied with four Syrian countries (Agusi, Melita, Gurgum and Kummuh). The Assyrians took many prisoners, and the Assyrian annals record that Sarduri himself fled under cover of night and was pursued by Tiglath-Pileser as far as the Euphrates crossing— that is, to the frontiers of his kingdom. The annals also record the rich booty captured in the Urartian camp, including a chariot, a bed, various valuables and a signet ring.

On this occasion the Assyrians contented themselves with the re-establishment of their authority in northern Syria and did not carry the war into Urartian territory. It was not until 735 that Tiglath-Pileser made up his mind to advance into Urartu. He met with no resistance on his way through the country, and came to Tushpa, where he laid siege to the fortress on the crag of Van, in which Sarduri had taken refuge. The annals written in the name of the Assyrian king record the event as follows: "I shut up Sarduri the Urartian in Turushpa (Tushpa), his principal city, and wrought great slaughter in front of the city gates. Then I set up the image of my majesty over against the city." The impregnable fortress on the rock withstood the siege, and the Assyrians, after destroying the town in the level country below, moved away. Tiglath-Pileser's victory was a blow to the power of Urartu, though not an irremediable one. With this weakening of Urartian authority, however, one region after another fell away, and Sarduri had to set about reconquering the territories which had been incorporated in the Urartian kingdom during the reign of his father Argishti.

The Reign of Rusa I

Our knowledge of the history of Urartu is still fragmentary, and for many periods we have no information from written sources. This is the case, for example, with the closing years of Sarduri's reign and the beginning of his son Rusa's.

Rusa became king at a time of great difficulty for the Kingdom of Van. He had not only to recover the territories which had been lost after the year 735, but found himself engaged in a stubborn struggle with the governors of the various regions, who sought from the very start of his reign to achieve independence; and at the same time he was compelled to provide for the defence of his country against Assyria.

We learn about this situation from a bilingual inscription set up on the pass between the Lake Urmia region and the country of Musasir. "Rusa, son of Sarduri, says: 'Urzana, king of the city of Ardini (Musasir), appeared before me. I took thought for the sustenance of all his army... Urzana I made governor of the region, establishing him in the city of Ardini. In the same year I, Rusa, son of Sarduri, came to the city of Ardini, and Urzana set me on the tall throne of the kings his ancestors... In the presence of the gods in the temple and in my presence he offered sacrifices... He put at my disposal auxiliary forces... and war chariots, as many as he had available. I took the auxiliary forces and in obedience to Haldi I, Rusa, went up into the mountains of Assyria and there did great slaughter. After this I took Urzana by the hand and concerned myself about him... I set him in the place of the sovereign so that he might rule.'" This extract makes it clear that for the Urartians Musasir was not merely a defensive position but a base from which to attack Assyria.

On succeeding to the throne Rusa, son of Sarduri, was compelled to concern himself not only with the defence of his frontiers but with the consolidation of his authority within Urartu itself, particularly in the peripheral areas. He reformed the regional administration, replacing the local governors by viceroys responsible to himself, and continued with the building of fortresses and towns; for many of the older centres had been destroyed during the Assyrian advance.

Only a few inscriptions by Rusa I have survived, and we cannot, therefore, conclude from the absence of any inscriptions bearing his name in the fortress on the crag of Van that the citadel of the capital had already been transferred to the hill of Toprakkale. The older centres in Transcaucasia also remained active. Objects of similar type (bronze shields, cups) with cuneiform inscriptions in the names of Argishti I, Sarduri II and Rusa I were found in the store-rooms of Erebuni, and also in the fortress of Teishebaini (Karmir-Blur) to which they had been transferred. In view of the growing threat from nomadic tribes, in particular the Cimmerians, who had already made their way through the Caucasian mountains into western Asia in the reign of Sarduri, Rusa devoted much attention to the Urartian centres in the north.

In the area round Lake Sevan he built two fortresses, one on the west of the lake ("the fortress of the god Haldi"), the other on the south ("the fortress of the god Teisheba"). The former was built on a high crag in the present-day town of Kamo (formerly Nor-Bayazed). A cuneiform inscription on a cornerstone recording its construction has survived: "Rusa, son of Sarduri, says: 'I conquered the king of the land of Uelikuhi, making him a slave, and drove him out of his country. Then I put a viceroy in his place, and I constructed the gates of the god Haldi and a mighty fortress, giving it the name of the fortress of the god Haldi.'" The land of Uelikuhi had been conquered in the reign of Sarduri II, but the governor had probably wavered in his loyalty during Urartu's time of trial and repressive action had therefore been necessary.

An inscription in a fortress near the present-day town of Tsovinar, which commanded the road round the south of the lake, records the defeat of 23 enemy countries in a single year and the building of the mighty fortress town of the god Teisheba "to declare the might of the land of Biaini and hold her enemies in awe."

In these difficult conditions of both internal and external strife Rusa I sought to maintain the power of his kingdom. He pursued an adroit foreign policy, avoiding any open clash with Assyria, now restored to its former strength, and seeking to preserve the security of his frontiers by treaties with the rulers of the neighbouring countries. Fortunately the Assyrian king, Shalmaneser V, was occupied with internal troubles and could spare little thought for Urartu. In the year 722 B.C., however, there was a sudden change in the situation, when Sargon, son of Tiglath-Pileser III, overthrew his brother and seized the Assyrian throne. From the very beginning of his reign Sargon showed a close interest in the course of events in neighbouring countries. In Syria and Palestine he was concerned by the activities of the petty princedoms which were supported by Egypt; in the south his objective was to bring Babylon into submission; and in the north he set out to destroy his ever-mighty foe, the kingdom of Urartu.

Sargon began by dealing with Syria and Palestine, defeating the forces of the Egyptian Pharaoh Shabaka, and then turned his attention to the northern front.

The Archives of the Assyrian Secret Service

We are well informed about the preparations for Sargon's campaign against Urartu by a remarkable collection of documents from the royal archives of Nineveh and Kalhu. These consist of reports from the Assyrian intelligence agents who were sent into enemy countries—small clay tablets covered with cuneiform, which a spy could readily conceal about his person, and sum-maries of these reports on larger tablets drawn up by the heir to the throne, Sennacherib, who acted as head of the intelligence service.

One of these agents, Uppahir-Bel, reports that he has "sent a special mes-senger to gather tidings from the land of Urartu" and has "kept watch from city to city, as far as Tushpa". Another, Gabbuana-Ashur, reports from a frontier fortress: "My messengers will go to Nabu-li, Ashur-bel-dan and Ashur-risua, who must perform their part. We have written down the names of all the men. Each one is carrying out his task; nothing has been neglected. We have heard many times that the Urartian king has not left Tushpa." It is interesting that the officers whose names appear in these reports conveyed the information they obtained direct to the Assyrian king. Thus among the tablets in the archives of Kuyunjik (Nineveh) there are eleven letters from Ashur-risua, and information communicated by him is quoted in eight letters from other correspondents.

From the reports of the Assyrian intelligence agents we learn of an unsuccessful campaign by the Urartians against the Cimmerians, in the course of which the leaders of the expedition, including the ruler of the district of Uasi (south-west of Lake Van), were killed, and of the disarray caused in Urartu by the defeat of their army. Ashur-risua devotes four letters to the revolt by the governors of Uasi and to the quelling of the rising by the Urartian king. But while Rusa was in Uasi another rising took place in his capital of Tushpa, led by his general Naragu. The letters tell how Rusa returned to Tushpa, captured the mutinous general and twenty officers who had joined the rising, and executed a hundred soldiers from the units which had come out in their support.

Having restored order in the country, Rusa turned to the strengthening of the Urartian frontiers and, having established a strong defensive line in the north, began a campaign of covert activity against Assyria. In the west he made a treaty with the ruler of the country of Tabal, Ambaris. Sargon reacted to this in 713 by sending his army against Tabal and bringing Ambaris back to Assyria as a prisoner. In the south Rusa increased his influence in Musasir by putting Urzana on the throne. Thereupon Sargon sent a threatening letter to Musasir, and Urzana had to make excuses for himself. In his reply he talks of neutrality and claims that the Assyrian demands are unjustified. There was also a determined struggle for influence in the country of Mannai, to the south of Lake Urmia. Sargon put his protégé Aza on the Mannaean throne; whereupon Rusa engineered a rebellion in the country and gave the throne to Ullusunu. In 716 Sargon sent an army into Mannai, easily defeated the new ruler, who had been left to his fate, pardoned him, and set up a figure of himself as a symbol of submission. In the following year Rusa organised another rebellion, and Sargon again marched against Mannai, carrying off the new king, Daiukku, to Hamath. In these various activities both parties were clearly playing with fire.

In the year 714 B.C. Sargon took decisive action against Urartu, sending his armies into the countries east of Lake Urmia in an operation which had long been contemplated. We are well informed about this campaign from a large clay tablet, now in the Louvre, containing a report to the god Ashur written in literary form. The concluding lines of the text name not only the author—Tabshar-Ashur, the writer of a number of intelligence reports—but also the scribe, "Nabu-Shalimshunu, the great royal scribe, principal sage and vizier of Sargon king of Assyria, eldest son of Harmakku, a royal scribe from Assur".

The information given by this text is supplemented by some reliefs found in a room in Sargon's palace at Dur-Sharrukin. Unfortunately only the reliefs in the south-western part of the room have survived. These relate to the end of the campaign, the capture of the town of Musasir, and very usefully complement and illustrate the corresponding part of the Louvre text.

Sargon's Campaign against Urartu

The Louvre text tells us that in the early summer of 714 the Assyrian army marched out of Kalhu with a great caravan of camels and asses, crossed the Upper and Lower Zab during the spate, and climbed into a range of almost impassable mountains. There is a vivid description of the densely forested

47

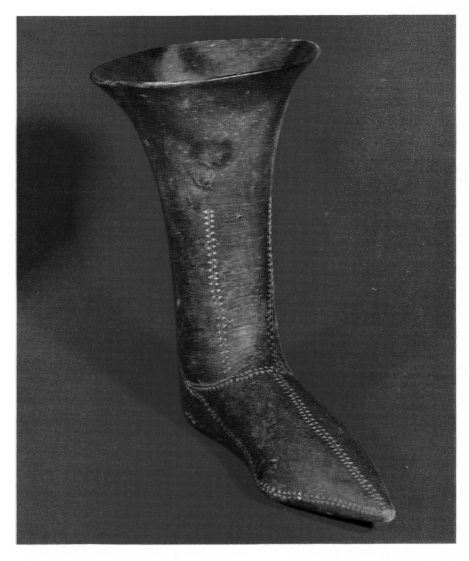

48

49

50, 51

58. 59

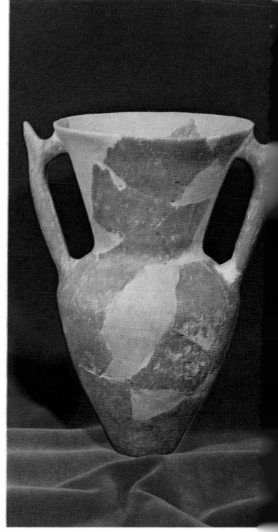

62, 63

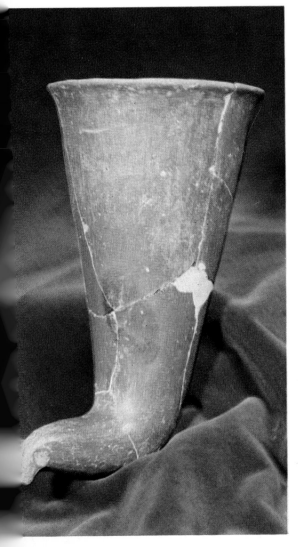
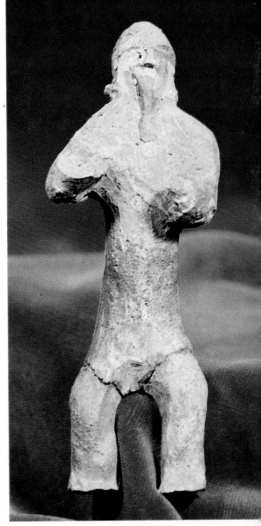

64, 65

69

mountains with their deep gorges into which the rays of the sun did not penetrate, and of the many rivers which had to be crossed, when the men of the army had to "fly over the water like eagles" and the camels and asses of the baggage train to "leap like mountain goats". After forcing six mountain passes and being ferried across two rivers, Sargon's army descended into the country of Mannai, where the Assyrian king received gifts from the rulers of the various districts. Sargon undertook that he would defeat the Urartians, free Mannai from their yoke and restore the former frontiers; but instead of moving to the north-west he turned east towards the countries of Zikirtu and Andi. Then, having stocked up the frontier fortresses with supplies, he advanced into Zikirtu; but the ruler of this country, Metatti, refused combat, abandoned his city of Parda and the treasures in his palace, and fled to the mountains.

Discontinuing the pursuit of the enemy, Sargon suddenly altered the direction of his advance. He had learned from an intelligence agent that Rusa and his allies, the leaders of the mountain tribes, had made their way round to his rear and had drawn up their battle array in the gorges of Mount Uaush (the present-day Mount Sahand). "My messenger made known to me the approach and the increase in number of their forces," records Sargon's account.

The correspondence in the Nineveh archives includes one letter in which it is tempting to see the messenger's report referred to in the Louvre text. In this document Bel-Iddin—evidently ruler of the country of Allabria which is mentioned in the Louvre text—has this to say about the Urartian king: "The messenger of the ruler of Andi and the messenger of the ruler of Zikirtu came to Uasi and said to him, 'The king of Assyria has come against us.' As soon as he had seen the messengers he set out for the land of Zikirtu. With his armies and the ruler of Hubha he continued for five days' march and then returned. To the magnates of his kingdom he said, 'Collect your warlike strength so that we may destroy the king of Assyria by taking him from the rear.'" It is an interesting point that this letter is written in bad Assyrian with grammatical and spelling mistakes.

Having received information about the position of the Urartian army, Sargon hastened into the country of Uishdish. He travelled in his war chariot, accompanied by a squadron of cavalry led by his intimate friend Sin-ahi-usur, whose palace stood next to the royal palace in Dur-Sharrukin. Then, without warning, he burst on the Urartian camp and utterly crushed them. The Urartian forces, archers and spearmen, were unable to withstand the attack, and "the mountain gorges were filled with their bodies and blood flowed like a river." Many of the cavalry, Urartian nobles, were taken prisoner. "On Mount Uaush I inflicted a defeat on the army of Urartu, my bitter enemy, and their allies, and put them to flight. With their horses I filled the mountain ravines and gorges, and they themselves, like ants in distress, departed by toilsome roads." Rusa himself, we are told, abandoned his war chariot and his charger and fled, mounted on a mare.

After inflicting this defeat on the Urartians in the land of Uishdish, Sargon's army advanced along the eastern shore of Lake Urmia in pursuit of the enemy, destroying fortresses, laying the whole area waste, and taking possession of the rich stores of grain in the granaries. Sargon then marched through the province of Subi, where riding horses were reared for the Urartian cavalry, and destroyed the city of Ulhu, described as an important centre of farming and horticulture.

The stone walls of the city were destroyed "like an earthen pot" and razed to the ground "with iron axes and swords". The palace suffered the same fate. The "brimming corn-bins of the city" and the wine-cellars were given over to the troops to plunder. The Assyrians "drew fragrant wine through clay pipes like river water." The outlet of the channel which brought drinking water to the city was blocked up and the area turned into a swamp. In all the surrounding countryside "the clangour of iron axes was heard", gardens were destroyed, and the felled trees were piled up and burned on the spot. The crops were destroyed to the last ear of grain, and the pasture land was trampled by the cavalry and the foot-soldiers.

Passing round Lake Urmia, Sargon's army now made for the north-eastern corner of Lake Van. They then seem to have marched past the capital city of Tushpa and continued round the northern and western shores of the lake: the exact route has not, however, been determined. Entering the land of Nairi, which lay to the south of Lake Van, on his return journey, Sargon decided to make a surprise attack on Musasir, the ruler of which, Urzana, was—as we have seen—an ally of the Urartian king.

Musasir was situated deep in the mountains. After a gruelling march the Assyrian army suddenly appeared outside the city and, "like locusts", spread over the whole countryside. The Louvre text gives a vivid description of the panic and confusion in the city, the sacrifices offered to Haldi to avert the calamity, and the assault, during which Sargon "caused the war-cry of his army to resound over the city like thunder." Urzana fled into the mountains, leaving his whole household behind him. Musasir was taken, and the Assyrians captured 6,110 prisoners, 380 asses, 525 cattle and 1,235 sheep. Sargon made a victorious entry into Urzana's palace and "seated himself on the throne like a sovereign."

The palace store-rooms were piled high with treasure. "The seals put on the doors for safe keeping were struck off", and their whole contents fell into Sargon's hands as booty. The text gives a long description of the captured wealth. Of gold alone there was rather more than a ton (34 talents and 18 minas), and of silver nearly five tons (167 talents and half a mina). In addition more than four hundred precious objects were taken from the palace; and the text enumerates 44 different types of object, including gold swords and daggers, Rusa's silver cups, cups from the land of Tabal with gold handles, and many other things.

Having taken possession of the treasure in the palace store-rooms, Sargon sent his retinue and the leaders of his army into the temple of Haldi, where there was still richer booty to be had. Here, in addition to a large quantity of gold (the exact amount is missing), the Assyrians captured another five tons of silver (162 talents and 20 minas, less a sixth of a mina) and more than 109 tons (3,600 talents) of bronze ingots.

Urartian Works of Art in Sargon's Booty

The text gives a detailed list of the valuables captured in the temple, mentioning 61 different items and a total of 333,500 objects in all. This catalogue is a document of exceptional importance for the study of the art and culture of Urartu. It notes, for example, the following items: "6 gold shields, flame-red in colour, which hung in his chamber on the right and left sides and shone with dazzling brightness; in the middle of them are the heads of dogs with bared teeth; they weighed 5 talents and 12 minas (about 14 lb)... 1 gold door-bolt in the form of a man's hand; the fastening of the door, on which is a winged monster; 1 gold peg for closing the bolt, to strengthen the lock of the temple and protect the riches amassed therein; 2 gold keys or bolts in the form of *lamassus* (winged demons) wearing tiaras, holding a curved sword and a hoop, and trampling on dogs with bared teeth. These four parts of the door-bolt, which were an ornament to the shrine and served to lock the doors, weighed 2 talents and 12 minas (about 145 lb) of gold."

On one of the reliefs from Sargon's palace—known only from a drawing by Flandin, since the original was lost in the Tigris while being shipped to France—was a scene showing the plundering of the temple at Musasir. This showed shields hanging on the pillars of the façade and in the spaces between them; and "in the middle of them are the heads of dogs with bared teeth." The Assyrians are shown carrying them off as booty, while a record is kept by an official sitting on a folding chair. In front of him stand two scribes, noting down the captured treasures—one of them in cuneiform on a clay tablet, the other in Aramaic script on a papyrus. The next scene shows the booty being weighed and taken away. It is difficult to reconstruct the complicated lock of the temple door as described in the Louvre text, but the excavators of a fortress at Hasanlu, to the south of Lake Urmia, found bronze pins from a lock, decorated with small figures of lions and attached to the door by a chain.

The custom of depositing weapons dedicated to the gods in their temples was widely practised in the ancient East. Since the principal Urartian gods were warrior gods, very large quantities of sacred and precious weapons were accumulated in their temples. It is not surprising, therefore, that in the temple at Musasir Sargon should have captured "25,212 brazen (or rather bronze) shields both heavy and light...; 1,514 brazen javelins both heavy and light; heavy brass spear-heads...; brass lances with brass supports; 305,412 swords..."

In addition to ordinary weapons the temple contained arms and equipment made of precious metal: "1 large sword, a weapon worn at his waist, to the making of which went 26 minas and 3 *su* (about 30 lb) of gold; 96 silver javelins; ...silver bows and silver spears, inlaid with gold and mounted; 12 heavy silver shields, the bosses of which are made in the form of the heads of monsters, lions and wild bulls...; 33 silver chariots."

The store-rooms also contained much valuable furniture, furnishings and jewellery, and this is again detailed in the list of booty: "393 silver cups, both heavy and light, made in Assyria, Urartu and Habhu; 2 horns of the great aurochs in a setting of gold circles; 1 gold signet ring with a seal for certifying the decrees of Bagmashtu, wife of Haldi, inlaid with precious stones; 9 fabrics for the clothing of his godhead, embroidered with golden discs; ...1 bed of ivory; 1 silver couch for the repose of his godhead, framed in gold and decorated with stones; 139 batons of ivory; ...10 tables of boxwood, and chairs of ebony and boxwood set with gold and silver; 2 altars; 14 various stones for the ornament of the divinity, precious stones belonging to Haldi and Bagmashtu his spouse..."

I have quoted only extracts from the inventory of the valuables captured by Sargon in Musasir, omitting many items which cannot yet be translated; but even this abbreviated list is enough to take our breath away. We should hardly have expected to find such an accumulation of treasures in the temple in Musasir, even allowing for the fact that Musasir was an ancient religious centre; and we find ourselves wondering whether the information given in the Louvre text is entirely trustworthy. It is fair to say, however, that we should have found it difficult to believe in the quantity of precious things in the tomb of the Pharaoh Tutankhamen if our only evidence had been an inventory recorded on a papyrus. It has also been suggested that Rusa might have sent the valuables stored in his treasury and his temples to Musasir in order to save them from the Assyrians. This, however, seems unlikely, since the journey to Musasir was long and hazardous and the area was always insecure in view of its nearness to Assyria. Moreover some details in the text indicate that the treasure belonged to Musasir. Thus there are two references to "Bagmashtu, wife of Haldi", and it is well established that the wife assigned to Haldi in central Urartu was Arubani. Evidently the goddess Bagmashtu, with her Iranian name, was an ancient divinity of Musasir, and when a new pantheon was established under Urartian influence she had perforce to become the wife of the supreme god.

The Louvre text also mentions a number of large bronze objects, some of which appear as decorations on the façade of the temple represented in the relief in Sargon's palace. These include "3 heavy brazen cauldrons, each with a capacity of 50 measures of water, and 1 large cauldron of a capacity of 80 measures, with a large brazen ladle, which the kings of Urartu filled with sacrificial wine when sacrifices were made to Haldi."

114

In a later passage the Louvre text enumerates some large pieces of brass (or rather bronze) sculpture which stood in the temple—examples of Urartian monumental art, about which otherwise we know nothing: "4 brazen statues of tall door-keepers, guardians of the temple door, and 4 supports which, together with the seat (pedestal), are of cast brass; 1 statue in an attitude of prayer, a representation of Sarduri, son of Ishpuini, king of Urartu, and his seat, of cast brass; 1 bull and 1 cow with its calf, cast by Sarduri, son of Ishpuini, who caused to be melted down (?) the brass of the temple of Haldi; 1 figure of Argishti, king of Urartu, crowned with the stellate tiara of divinity, with his right hand raised in blessing, together with its receptacle, of a weight of 60 talents (about 1 ton 16 cwt) of brass; 1 figure of Ursa (Rusa) with his two horses and his driver's horse, with their seat (pedestal), cast in brass, on which can be read the king's boast, 'With my two horses and my driver's horse my hand conquered the kingdom of Urartu.'"

Some of these pieces of sculpture can be seen in the relief from Sargon's palace. On each side of the entrance to the temple stand two of the four statues of "tall door-keepers", and to the right of the entrance is the cow with its calf "cast by Sarduri, son of Ishpuini"; there is no sign of the bull mentioned in the Louvre text. At the base of the platform, apparently on either side of the steps, are two huge cauldrons supported on tripods. Two similar cauldrons were found in the excavations of the fortress of Teishebaini (Karmir-Blur), the cauldrons themselves being wrought from brass sheet and the rims cast in bronze (Plate 70).

The inscription on the pedestal of the statue of Rusa referring to his conquest of the kingdom of Urartu has inevitably attracted the interest of historians. It has been suggested, for example, that Rusa was not the son of his predecessor Sarduri but a usurper, the founder of a new dynasty. But this is in contradiction with the reference to "Rusa, son of Sarduri" in the king's inscriptions; and in any case if Rusa had really not been the legitimate heir to the throne the Assyrian annals would certainly have mentioned this, as they always did when referring to usurpers. A more likely explanation is that the inscription on Rusa's statue referred to the restoration of the earlier frontiers of the Urartian kingdom and the reconquest of the countries which had taken advantage of the weakening of central authority after Tiglath-Pileser's campaigns against Urartu to assert their independence.

The Louvre text also gives us some conception of Urartian monumental sculpture, of which hardly any actual examples have survived. Of smaller work we have only three bronze statuettes of divinities—the only specimens which chance has preserved. These are a figurine of a bearded god wearing a tiara decorated with horns, now in the British Museum; a figurine of a seated goddess, probably Arubani, in the National Historical Museum of Armenia; and a statuette of the god Teisheba (?) found in the excavations at Karmir-Blur *(Plate 106)*. The only piece of large sculpture in stone which has survived is a badly damaged basalt statue (height of the surviving part 4 feet 2 inches), now in the Museum of Georgia in Tbilisi. Its upper part was known as early as 1898, and the remainder came to light later, following an explosion in the fortress on the crag of Van. Originally the statue was roughly life size. The headdress and the face are missing, but it is just possible to distinguish the wavy hair, falling down the back and shoulders, and the beard. The absence of the headdress makes it impossible to determine whether the figure represents a king or a god. He holds a club or whip and a bow and arrows, and a sword hangs at his side; but these weapons could be carried either by a king or by a god.

But let us return to the bronze statues in the temple at Musasir. We do not know what happened to them after the capture of the town. It is highly unlikely that they could be transported to Assyria through almost impassable mountain country. On the relief from Sargon's palace, next to the scene showing the looting of the temple, we see the booty being weighed and the various objects being carried away; and nearby are three Assyrian soldiers breaking

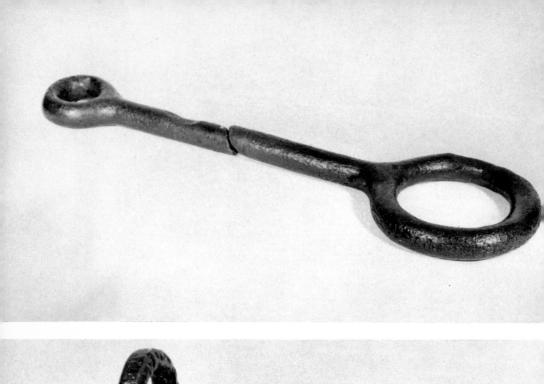

74

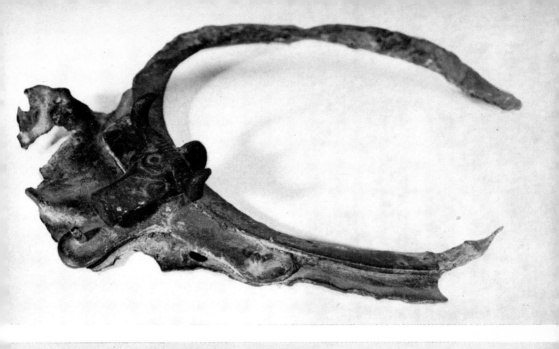

75, 76

up a statue with axes — one of the pieces of bronze sculpture described in Sargon's report to the god Ashur.

Thus thanks to the remarkable literary text recovered from the ruins of Assur, the Assyrian capital, and to the narrative reliefs from Sargon's palace at Dur-Sharrukin, we are well informed about this episode in the military history of Assyria and are able to glean much information about the culture of Urartu.

The campaign for which Sargon had made such meticulous preparations was thus crowned with success; and the Assyrian annals record laconically that "when Ursa (Rusa), king of Urartu, heard that Musasir had been destroyed and his god Haldi carried away, then with his own hand, with the iron dagger which hung at his side, he put an end to his life."

Argishti II and the Recovery of Urartu: the Finds at Altıntepe

The utter defeat which Urartu suffered at the hands of Sargon in 714 B.C. did not destroy the Kingdom of Van. After the death of Rusa I his son Argishti II succeeded to the throne and at once bent his energies to making good the devastations of the war. Once again Sargon was compelled to keep a watchful eye on developments in Urartu. Among the letters from intelligence agents in this period is a report on the arrival in Harda, a frontier town in the upper Tigris Valley (near the modern town of Diyarbakır), of a messenger from Argishti countermanding a previous order from the king and giving instructions to look after his horses until the arrival of a second messenger. There is also an account of a dispute in the forest over some logs which the Urartians would not allow the Assyrians to take away; and a third letter reports that Urartian forces have already advanced to the town of Harda.

Thus the young Urartian king was clearly not of a mind to lay down his arms, but was continually seeking to consolidate his authority, not least on his western frontier. It took Sargon until 708 B.C., six years after his campaign against Urartu, to deal with the king of Kummuh, who paid an annual tribute to Argishti II as the price of his support.

In the last years of Sargon's reign his attention was diverted from the north, and after his death a confused political situation developed in Assyria. There may even have been attempts at a *coup d'état*, as we learn from letters in the Nineveh archives — documents of exceptional interest, since they furnish us with information from a non-official source to supplement the meagre evidence available in the Assyrian annals.

The Urartian kingdom was thus granted a breathing space and was able to rally after its defeat. From the cuneiform inscriptions we learn of intense building activity by Argishti in the central part of the kingdom, particularly in the areas through which Sargon's army had passed. On a site near the modern town of Erciş, on the northern shores of Lake Van, he built the town of Titumnia, laying out an artificial lake and digging a canal. In this area there are a number of ancient fortresses, and some outstanding works of art have been found here. It is possible also that a large relief carved on several blocks of stone representing the god Teisheba standing on a bull — apparently a figure from a procession — dates from this period and comes from some monumental structure which has not survived. At the same time as he was building these new towns and fortresses Argishti also began the construction of another new town at Tushpa, on the hill of Toprakkale — an enterprise which was to be completed by his son.

Argishti, son of Rusa, seems to have been king of Urartu throughout the reign of Sennacherib, Sargon's son (704–681), but the Assyrian annals of this period are silent about events in Urartu. Sennacherib was preoccupied with wars against Babylon, Syria and Palestine, and also with preparations

for a campaign against Egypt: he therefore avoided open war with his northern neighbour, although at this period the Urartian frontier was not far
removed from the centre of Assyria. On the evidence of Sennacherib's
inscriptions, Mount Tas (the present-day Mount Bavian), where the Assyrian
king had a hunting park, lay "on the frontier of Urartu". Near the frontier,
too, was a large aqueduct, carried on high walls and arches, which brought
water from the mountains into Nineveh. As we have already noted, however,
the mountains of Kurdistan, which separated the Lake Van basin from
central Assyria, were almost impassable and constituted a secure natural
barrier.

Argishti II was particularly concerned to strengthen his distant frontiers. A
powerful frontier fortress was established on the banks of the upper Euphrates, near Erzincan. Here, on the mound of Altıntepe, systematic excavations by Turkish archaeologists have revealed the remains of a large
fortress defended by massive walls, the name of which is still unknown.
Within the fortress a number of buildings have been excavated, including a
small "*susi*" temple similar in plan to the one on Arin-Berd, but differing
from it in being situated in the centre and not on one side of a colonnaded
courtyard. The foundations of the temple are built of carefully dressed
basalt blocks; the walls, constructed of adobe brick, have not survived, but
remains of wall painting were found in the rubble. On a dais inside the temple
was a sacrificial altar, and another altar was found standing in the open in
front of four tall round-topped stelae. An Urartian seal impression which
came to light many years ago shows a sacrifice being performed in front of
three similar stelae and a sacred tree.

This fortress was the residence of the Urartian viceroy, who occupied a
position of great dignity and importance, and under the walls of the fortress
were the tombs of persons of high rank, similar in form to the royal tombs
hewn in the crag of Van. Two of these, built in large blocks of stone, contained three chambers, and in their walls were niches of the same type as in

the Horhor Cave with the inscription by Argishti I. The entrances to the tombs were closed by large stone slabs. In one of the chambers were two sarcophagi with lids of semicircular section carved from single blocks of stone. Excavation of the tombs yielded much interesting material, including elements from furniture, made of bronze and wood and inlaid with discs of horn, which have made it possible to reconstruct couches with feet in the form of bulls' hooves, decorated with wreaths formed of petals.

Other items which have attracted much attention are a bronze cauldron decorated with bulls' heads, supported on a tripod, other bronze vessels including one with a Hittite inscription, and a shield.

The tombs also contained many bronze and iron weapons, a bronze shield, harness fittings and a bit decorated with horses' heads, and bronze belts with figures of horsemen and winged bulls. There were also some interesting pieces of jewellery, consisting of gold buttons and a plaque with granulated decoration. Many of the objects found — characteristic examples of Urartian art in the first half of the 8th century B.C. — belong to the reign of Argishti II, as is indicated by inscriptions bearing his name on some of the items. It is to be hoped that further excavation on Altıntepe (the "golden mound") will bring to light further cuneiform inscriptions to supplement our meagre information about the course of events in this period.

Assyria in Difficulties: the Reign of Rusa II

The Assyrian King Sennacherib was killed in 681 B.C. in a palace revolution, and after the accession of Esarhaddon (681–668 B.C.) his murderers fled to the north-west, to the land of Shupria, which bordered on Urartu. The Old Testament preserves a recollection of this, recording that Sennacherib's sons, having killed their father, fled to Urartu (the "land of Ararat" or "land of Armenia").

The Assyrian written sources do not enable us to put a date on the end of Argishti's reign, though in texts belonging to the time of Esarhaddon — unfortunately undated — we find references to a new Urartian king called Rusa, son of Argishti.

At this period the Assyrians were threatened by a new danger which was now looming up. This was the advance of the nomadic tribes — the Cimmerians (Gimirraya) and the Scythians (Ashguzaya) — who were penetrating into western Asia through the Caucasus. Although the annals record victories over the nomads — in particular over "Teushpa the Cimmerian from a distant land" and the army of the Scythian Ishpaka, who was allied with the country of Mannai — the Assyrians nevertheless sought to enlist these formidable enemies on their side. Among the oracles of Esarhaddon — questions addressed to the god Shamash and recorded on clay tablets — is one in which he asks whether the king of the Scythians, Partatua, will remain loyal to his alliance if, as he asks, he is given an Assyrian princess in marriage. The answer to the questions have not been preserved, and we do not know whether proposed marriage ever took place. In a legal document of 679 B.C., however, there is a reference to a certain Ishdi-Harran, "commander of the Scythian regiment" — evidently a regiment of mercenaries.

The situation of Assyria took a turn for the worse when the northern nomads began to enter into alliances with other countries — including, for example, Urartu. Assyrian apprehensions at these developments were well founded. Esarhaddon asked Shamash whether the plans of Rusa, king of the Urartians, and of the Cimmerians would be realised: would they move into the land of Shupria? This was the turbulent country to which Sennacherib's murderers had fled and which had also provided asylum for "Urartian refugees".

The Cimmerians' advance brought them to the region round Lake Van, where they settled for a considerable period. A letter in the Nineveh archives tells of operations against the Cimmerians in the country of Maki, and of the preparation of ambushes in the mountain passes; another gives instructions about the surveillance of the frontiers of Urartu, Mannai, Media and Hubushkia and about the treatment of deserters, who are to be sent immediately to the crown prince's palace. Rusa II maintained friendly relations with the nomads, and the excavations of the fortress of Teishebaini, the Urartian military and administrative centre in Transcaucasia, have produced evidence of close links between the Urartians and the Scythians which would ensure the security of the northern frontiers. The excavators of Teishebaini discovered a number of Scythian objects (weapons, pieces of harness, ornaments) not only from the northern Caucasus but from the more distant Dnieper area.

On the evidence of the written sources and the surviving archaeological remains the reign of Rusa II seems to have been a period of intense building activity, a time when Urartu reasserted its position among the nations of western Asia. In the west Rusa directed his efforts towards the re-establishment of Urartian control over the routes to the Mediterranean, and one of his inscriptions refers to the capture of prisoners in the countries of Mushkini, Hatti and Halittu, which lay on and beyond the Euphrates. Unfortunately an inscription by Rusa in the western territories, in the fortress of Mazgerd, is badly damaged and cannot be read.

In central Urartu, at Tushpa, Rusa completed the construction of the town on the hill of Toprakkale, giving it the name of Rusahinili. He built up his capital into a flourishing area extending from the crag of Van to the mountain ridge on which he had constructed his new royal residence, providing water channels, creating an artificial lake, planting gardens and vineyards, and laying out fields for cultivation. An inscription recording the development of the capital notes particularly that the water channels were intended to serve the needs both of the new city of Rusahinili and of Tushpa. Much archaeological work has been done on the citadel of Toprakkale, beginning in 1879 and continuing to the present day, and most of the best known examples of Urartian art which have found their way into museums through commercial channels come from here.

The excavations on Toprakkale have revealed the remains of a palace decorated with a polychrome stone mosaic formed of large pieces of stone of diamond, rectangular or swallowtail shape. The basalt slabs of the floor and the wall surfaces were also decorated with large concentric pieces of white, red and black stone *(Plate 16)* inserted in cavities cut in the stone or the bronze sheets on the walls. In spite of the destruction caused by the trenching of the treasure-hunters, the excavations of recent years have brought to light various domestic offices, including wine-cellars containing large jars *(pithoi)* sunk into the earth floor.

Archaeologists have also long been interested in the *"susi"* temple, of a type frequently found in Urartu, consisting of a single chamber with a paved area in front of the entrance. Recently, while investigating the corners of the temple, the archaeologists found under them four square cavities, in two of which were bronze plaques, unfortunately without inscriptions. On each plaque was a small diamond-shaped piece of gold leaf and a rectangle of silver leaf, the symbolism of which is unexplained. It may be that other Urartian buildings will be found to contain tablets with foundation inscriptions similar to those discovered in buildings in Assyria and Achaemenid Iran. Near the temple were found a number of large ornamental bronze shields with figures of bulls and lions. Most of the shields had inscriptions in the name of one of the last Urartian kings, Rusa, son of Erimena, but one of them bore the name of Rusa, son of Argishti — suggesting that Rusa II was the builder of the temple but that Rusa III restored it and deposited in it pieces of sacred armour dedicated to Haldi.

Rusahinili remained the residence of the Urartian kings for something like a hundred years. It was destroyed at the beginning of the 6th century B.C. by the Medes, who dealt the final blow to the Kingdom of Van.

Building Activity in Urartu in the 7th Century B. C.

In all the large centres founded by Argishti II, his son Rusa II left foundation inscriptions and continued the building operations which his father had begun. At Adılcevaz some large foundation and sacrificial inscriptions by Rusa II were found, and the fortress on the hill of Kefkalesi must also be dated to his reign. Here the excavators cleared various structures forming part of a large building with pylons constructed of large blocks of dressed basalt, and also a number of separate rectangular blocks — the bases of columns, which themselves would be built of adobe brick. The column bases were decorated with carvings representing two winged bulls standing on lions against the background of a building with battlements and towers similar to the tall building on the bronze plaque found at Toprakkale. The composition of the carvings is a rather clumsy combination of different elements. Instead of the usual stylised tree, as on the carving of Teisheba from Adılcevaz, there are three small trees in front of the towers, and in consequence the attitude of the god fertilising the sacred tree seems a little unnatural. Above, on the merlons of the battlements, is a palmette between two birds holding a rabbit in their beaks.

The peripheral fortress at Altıntepe also continued to exist in Rusa II's reign. Objects found here had inscriptions in his name, and many pieces of applied art showed affinities with material found at Toprakkale. Of particular interest are some ivory plaques showing winged genii with eagles' heads which recall the bone carvings found in great quantity and variety at Kalhu.

On the north-eastern frontier, near the modern town of Manu in Iran, was built a fortress named "King Rusa's small city", as we know from the chance finding of an inscription on a stone from its walls.

Of Rusa's large-scale building operations in the territory north of the Araxes eloquent evidence is provided by the citadel of the city of Teishebaini, the remains of which have been found on the mound of Karmir-Blur (Erevan). The story of the excavation of this fortress is told in the next chapter: here it is necessary to note only a few general points. The citadel of Teishebaini occupied a total area of some 10 acres and contained some 150 separate apartments together with a spacious courtyard. The whole structure is remarkable for its massive strength, with walls ranging between 7 and 12 feet in thickness, and its considerable height of up to 24 feet. Most of the buildings were roofed with a barrel vault of adobe brick; some had roofs formed of large beams of pine, poplar, beech and other types of timber. The building of the citadel required some 2 million large adobe bricks (20 inches long by 14 inches thick); the total quantity of timber required — most of it brought from other areas — cannot be estimated. Thus the construction of the citadel involved a vast expenditure of labour on the making and laying of the bricks, the transport of the timber, the quarrying and dressing of the stone used in the foundations and the basalt blocks employed in the architectural decoration of the upper storey. It is clear that a colossal building effort of this kind demanded a very large labour force, most probably provided by prisoners taken in war.

The citadel of Teishebaini contained eight wine-stores with a total capacity of some 9,000 gallons, small store-rooms for grain arranged along both sides of a corridor, with a total capacity of some 750 tons — and at least as much again was stored in granaries elsewhere in the citadel. Figures of this kind give some idea of the power of the Urartian kingdom in the 7th century B.C. Only a high productive capacity and a securely established political position could have enabled the Urartians to build such a mighty fortress as this in Transcaucasia. And we know that in fact the political position of Urartu in this period was secure. The Assyrians were careful to avoid any clash with the Urartians, and the Urartians sought likewise to give no occasion for conflict.

In the year 654 B.C., after Ashurbanipal's victory over King Teuman o Elam and capture of Susa, Rusa II sent emissaries to the Assyrian king. "At this time," record the Assyrian annals, "Rusa, king of Urartu, heard of the mightiness of my gods and was overcome by terror at my majesty. Then he sent his princes to Arbela to bring me greetings." And in the reliefs from the palace in Nineveh we can see the Urartian envoys among those present at the savage torturing and execution of the Elamites.

There was a second Urartian mission to Ashurbanipal in the year 639 B.C., after his war against the Arabs, but this time it was sent by a different king — Sarduri, son of Rusa.

THE CITY OF TEISHEBA
(KARMIR-BLUR)

IV

The Site and the Excavations

Thirty years ago, if the inhabitants of Erevan had been asked about Karmir-Blur, they might have replied that it was a hill on the outskirts of the town *(Plates 17, 20)*, on the left bank of the River Razdan, easily seen from the road to Echmiadzin, the residence of the Armenian Catholicos — a favourite place with sportsmen, the haunt of many migrant birds, of hares, and perhaps of an occasional fox. Some of them might have added that there had once been a mediaeval bell-tower on the hill, but that this had now disappeared.

If the same question were put to the inhabitants of Erevan today, the reply would be that Karmir-Blur is in the western part of the town, that an ancient city has been excavated here, and that one room in the Historical Museum of Armenia is full of interesting material from the site belonging to the ancient kingdom of Urartu.

Karmir-Blur first attracted the attention of archaeologists in 1936, when there was found on the slopes of the hill a broken piece of stone from a wall with fragmentary remains of a cuneiform inscription containing the name of Rusa II. This suggested that the hill concealed the remains of a fortress belonging to the period of Urartian resurgence.

The systematic excavation of Karmir-Blur *(Plates 17–33)* began in 1939, and has been carried on by a joint expedition sponsored by the Academy of Science of the Armenian SSR and the Hermitage Museum. The expedition has had as its objective to make a complete study of the fortress on the hill and to excavate the districts of the town lying on three sides of the hill. (To the north and north-east the face of the hill descends steeply to the gorge of the Razdan.)

Karmir-Blur was slow to reveal its secrets, but the investigation of the site is now almost complete. Much information has been gathered by the patient efforts of the excavators, but chance has also played its part in the discoveries.

At the start of their work the archaeologists were puzzled by the complete absence of the sherds of pottery which are normally found on ancient inhabited sites. Karmir-Blur was quite devoid of any such remains. On the first day of excavation, however, fragments of brickwork began to appear, and the excavators set about tracing the line of the walls which could be seen emerging from the ground. But the work was laborious, and it was often difficult to know where to look next. Then work was brought to a standstill by heavy rain; and on the following morning the whole layout of the fortress was visible on the ground. The walls of adobe brick retained the water longer than the earth filling and showed up clearly as darker outlines on the ground. At Uruk in southern Mesopotamia — so we are told — the "Hall of Cere-monies" (Bit-Akitu) outside the city was discovered in the same way. In this case the excavators first saw the outline of the building by moonlight, but could no longer distinguish it the following day; and it was only after a downpour of rain that traces of the walls again became visible on the wind-smoothed surface of the desert.

The archaeologists were long unable to establish the layout of the ancient settlement round Karmir-Blur, since the whole area had been dug over by the local inhabitants in their quest for building stone. But when the site was photographed from the air the whole plan of the town could be seen at a glance, with its pattern of longitudinal and cross streets. The photographs thus provided a useful guide for further excavation.

The excavation of the citadel began with a small room to some 215 square feet. The lines of the walls were clearly marked, and the soft earth filling was easily removed; but the room went down to an unusual depth, so that it seemed more like a well than a room. As excavation continued small door-ways were revealed in two of the walls, and finally, at a depth of 23½ feet, the floor was reached. Nothing was found in the room, however, but one broken jug of polished red pottery.

The unusual depth of the rooms, which were filled with a mass of brick rubble from the walls *(Plate 33)*, and the absence of any level containing evidence of occupation puzzled the archaeologists and suggested the possibility that the fortress had remained unfinished and that the other rooms would also turn out to be empty. Further excavation, however, revealed some rather better furnished rooms, and a variety of objects — wooden vessels, scraps of cloth, raisins, pieces of bread, a pomegranate flower — were found buried under the debris; and it was seen that the brick rubble, forming a thick layer impervious to moisture and to air, had preserved organic remains which normally disappear without leaving any trace.

Before beginning the systematic excavation of the rooms in the citadel it was necessary to determine the plan of the whole building. This was a straightforward but laborious operation. A trench 6 feet wide was driven along the line of the wall footings, and each day's excavation made its contribution to filling in the details of the plan. After three years' work this showed a fortress with large square towers and buttresses at intervals along the walls *(Plates 22–24)*, and with a number of square projections in the wall overlooking the river. On the west side of the citadel was a large courtyard, entered by the massive and strongly defended South Gate and by a more lightly defended postern gate in the north-west corner. Here again, however, a surprise awaited the archaeologists. They had discovered entrances into the courtyard, but the main citadel building had no gate: a massive stone wall 6 feet high ran round the entire perimeter. It was not until later that the meaning of this structure was explained, and the fortress on Karmir-Blur was shown to be an interesting example of ancient Oriental architecture.

A characteristic feature of the palaces of Assyria was the platform of adobe brick on which they were built. In the case of Sargon's palace this reached

137

a height of 45 feet. Assyrian foundation inscriptions give us detailed accounts of the method of construction of these platforms. In Assyrian buildings there were as a rule no rooms within the platform, which normally contained only barrel-vaulted channels which served for drainage. In the citadel of Karmir-Blur, however, the ground floor, containing store-rooms and domestic offices, also served as the "platform" on which the upper floor was built. The rooms on the ground floor could be entered only from above. Some of them were completely cut off from the rest; and those on which the massive superstructure was to be built — the actual "platform" — were packed with a solid mass of stone. The entrance to the citadel was by means of a ramp on the south-western side, the position of which is revealed by the present slope of the hill.

Workshops and Store-Rooms

The upper floor contained 148 rooms of different sizes and functions, ranging from small store-rooms *(Plates 30, 33)* to extensive warehouses and workshops. The various rooms were built out at different levels according to the contours of the hill, and the windows of the rooms in the middle were placed high up in the wall under the ceiling, presumably looking out over the roofs of the lower parts of the building. A stepped arrangement of this kind is characteristic of the architecture of Mesopotamia.

The rooms in the citadel were designed for a variety of purposes. Three large rooms in the north-east corner, for example, were devoted to the production of sesame oil. In one of them was found a large tufa vat used for soaking the grain before pressing. On the floor of the second room was a considerable quantity of sesame oilcake, the residue left after production of the oil; the wooden press which had stood in this room had been totally consumed by fire. The third room, in which the oil had been stored *(Plate 30)*, showed traces of a fierce fire which had reduced the adobe brick of the walls to clinker.

There was also a brewhouse for the production of beer, with a stone vat containing traces of malted barley. The beer brewed here was kept in large round-bottomed jars of elongated shape *(Plate 57)*.

Two other rooms had been used for the working of stagshorn. Lying about the floor were horns, sawn-off pieces of horn, and iron saws.

Outside the citadel were potters' and metalsmiths' workshops. Since the firing of pottery and the smelting of metal involved particular fire risks, these processes were carried on in special buildings at a safe distance from the living quarters. The citadel also contained store-rooms for dishes and vessels of various kinds: in one were wine jugs *(Plates 49, 50)*, in another jars and bowls for milk, in a third domestic pottery. In many rooms were found metal objects in process of manufacture and bronze ingots of irregular shape, with one side flat and the other convex.

Many rooms were used for the storage of grain. In the western part of the citadel were a number of small store-rooms laid out along both sides of a corridor; but grain was also stored in other parts of the building. Large stocks of wheat, barley and millet were found *(Plate 29)* — grain of high quality with only a small admixture of tares. An interesting detail was the discovery of the remains of pests — weevils and ants — which had preyed on the Urartian grain.

We know from inscriptions the high standard of agriculture practised in the area round Teishebaini. A large stele found in the Zvarthnots temple, near Echmiadzin, which probably once stood on the right bank of the Razdan opposite Karmir-Blur, has the following inscription: "Rusa, son of Argishti, says: 'In the valley of the land of Kuturlini the soil had never been worked. Then on the command of Haldi I planted this vineyard, and laid out sown fields all round, encircling the cities with them. I led a water channel from the River Ildaruni: its name is Umeshini.'" There follow instructions about the offering of sacrifices to the gods in honour of the inauguration of the channel. The great importance which the Urartian kings attached to irrigation works is evident from this text; and the water channel of Umeshini — a large tunnel bored through the heart of the andesite and basalt rock — still survives after 2600 years, bearing eloquent testimony to the scale on which these works were carried out *(Plate 31)*.

The excavators of the citadel also found the remains of various kinds of fruit — plums *(Plate 26)*, grapes of different sorts, apples, quinces, cherries and pomegranates. An important part in the economy of Teishebaini was played by the wine-stores, of which there were six. These were large rooms, usually unlighted, in which rows of large jars *(pithoi)* were sunk into the ground, each with its capacity indicated in cuneiform or hieroglyphs. The capacity of the jars ranged between 17½ and 26½ gallons, and since the total number of jars in all the store-rooms was about 400 — the jars in two of the rooms being largely destroyed — the total quantity of wine in store must have been about 9,000 gallons. This is much in excess of the quantity stored in other fortresses for which this information is given in inscriptions.

The store-rooms were damp and dark, as is shown by the finding of large numbers of oil lamps, with holes for the wick, and by such unexpected discoveries as a wasps' nest in the corner of one room and the skeleton of a toad near one of the wine-jars. The store-rooms had timber roofs, the pinewood beams of which were so well preserved that a local violin-maker was able to use a piece of the wood to make the sounding-board of a violin which was played by a member of the Erevan Philharmonic Orchestra.

There was also a large wine-store on the upper floor in the southern part of the citadel. This may have been used for sweet wines which had to be matured in the sun.

Near the wine-cellars were found store-rooms containing jugs for dispensing the wine. In one of these were 1,036 jugs of polished red pottery, more than

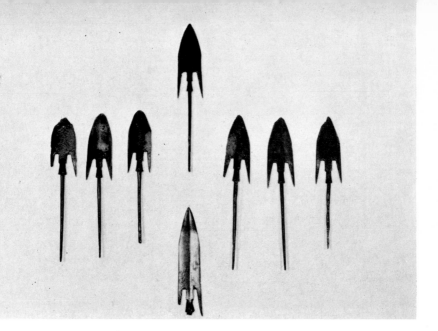

84

87

85, 86   88

89, 90   91

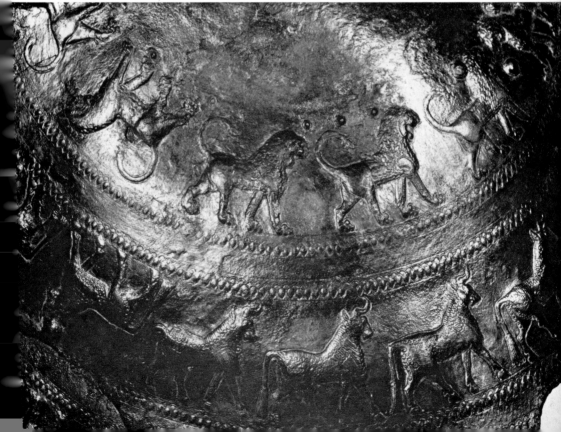

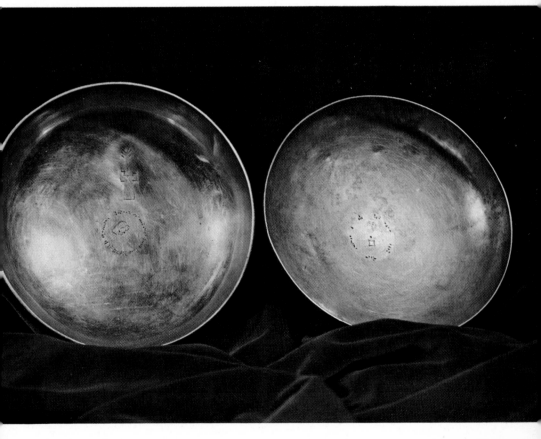

a hundred of them being completely intact. In another room near the wine-cellars were a large number of bronze cups, unfortunately in a poor state of preservation. In a wine-cellar on the west side of the citadel, however, 87 bronze cups were found stacked up in one of the wine-jars for safe keeping. Most of these cups *(Plates 97, 98)* had preserved their original lustre and still gave out a melodious tone when struck. In the centre of each was a stamped cuneiform inscription bearing the name of one of the 8th century Urartian kings — Menua, Argishti I, Sarduri II or Rusa I. On many of them was an emblem in the form of a fortified tower and a tree.

The Name of the Fortress

In many of the store-rooms remains of the doors were found. These were made of thick planks of wood and were locked by means of a hinged bronze latch. On one of these a brief cuneiform inscription was found in 1945: "The fortress (literally 'armoury') of the city of Teishebaini, belonging to King Rusa, son of Argishti" *(Plate 74)*. This inscription confirmed the theory that the fortress on Karmir-Blur had been built in the 7th century B.C. and named after Teisheba, the god of war, of storms and of thunder: it was Teishebaini, the city of Teisheba. Since the inscription was found on a small object the possibility remained that it might originally have come from another fortress—perhaps on the southern shore of Lake Sevan, where Rusa had built another town named after Teisheba. The name of the fortress was finally confirmed in 1962, when the excavators discovered in the southern part of the citadel a pile of large blocks of stone from the foundations of a temple on which were two long cuneiform inscriptions. The first inscription begins with the statement that King Rusa, son of Argishti, has built a *susi* temple in honour of Haldi and the splendid Gate of Haldi in the city of Teishebaini, situated in the land of Aza. It then goes on to record that the area had previously been a desert, and that on succeeding to the throne Rusa II had erected the buildings to which the inscription related. In honour of the work certain sacrifices to Urartian gods and goddesses were prescribed — bulls, kids and sheep to the gods, cows to the goddesses. The concluding part of the inscription lays down the sacrifices that are to be made to the king when he comes to Teishebaini.

Thus this inscription, found in the final stage of the excavations, in their twenty-second year, confirmed all the conclusions reached by the archaeologists about the fortress on Karmir-Blur. Like Erebuni and Argishtihinili, it was situated in the land of Aza. The inscription follows, word for word, the formulae used in the foundation inscriptions at Armavir (Argishtihinili) and Adılcevaz. It indicates that Teishebaini was built at the beginning of Rusa II's reign, and that the king himself was accustomed to visit this important centre of administration and economic life north of the Araxes. The fortress was occupied by a military garrison and was the headquarters of the viceroy and the seat of the Urartian administration. Tribute from the surrounding area was sent to Teishebaini, processed in the workshops of the fortress, and then despatched to the central part of the kingdom.

Stock-Rearing and Animal Sacrifices

The large scale on which sacrifice was performed here is confirmed by archaeological evidence. The excavators found one room filled with the burned bones of young calves and smaller animals. The skulls and lower extremities were missing — a feature which is paralleled in sacrifices of animals in the Caucasus.

In 1965 a room was excavated in which the choicest parts (the neck and part of the breast) of 26 cattle carcasses had been laid out. Nothing was, of course, left but the bones, which lay in correct anatomical arrangement, many of them showing the marks of the axe. It seems probable that this was not a store of meat for domestic consumption but a collection of pieces destined for sacrifice.

Urartian stock-rearing activities are well represented at Teishebaini, not only by separate bones left over from meat which had been eaten but also by the complete skeletons of animals which had perished in the fire. At the time of the siege and of the conflagration which accompanied the storming of the fortress the animals — cattle, horses and asses — were on the roof of the north-western part of the citadel. When the timber roofing became enveloped in flames the animals broke loose from their halters and rushed about in panic, found their way on to a part of the roof where the timber had been consumed by the fire, and fell through to the floor below. The excavations produced much evidence — the position of the skeletons and their damaged condition — to indicate that the animals had fallen from a considerable height. The remains found included not only bones but also carbonised fragments of flesh and skin, as well as parts of the entrails and the contents of the animals' stomachs *(Plate 27)*. In one stomach the undigested remains of plants and water-melon seeds could be clearly distinguished.

The cattle, of which a number of skeletons were found, were of a type very similar to *Bos primigenius*. Dairy farming was highly developed in Urartu, and the excavations at Teishebaini yielded a number of large churns with wedges fitted to the internal surface to speed up the butter-making process. That cheese was also produced is suggested by the finding of a small double jar containing a caked mass of organic matter, including grain. After careful analysis it was suggested, very plausibly, that the vessel had contained a curdling agent for making cheese compounded from a piece of tissue from an animal's stomach, some grains of sorghum and raisins. A similar substance is still used in cheese-making in our own day.

The smaller animals found included two types of sheep, one of them (merino) being remarkable for the high quality of its wool.

One of the accounting documents *(Plate 36)* found at Teishebaini contains a record of 224 calves' hides, 52 skeins of wool, 172 sheepskins and 18 goat-skins.

The technique of working wool has been known in western Asia since the remotest times. In the store-rooms of Teishebaini were found many skeins of woollen yarn, spindles with yarn, and odd pieces and cuts of woollen cloth of different qualities, some of them still with a well preserved nap.

We know that costly woollen fabrics, dyed in many colours, were manu-factured in Urartu: this is indicated by various Assyrian texts, in particular by Sargon's account of the capture of the temple at Musasir, which refers to "130 many-coloured garments and tunics of flax and blue and purple wool from the lands of Urartu and Habhu". Unfortunately the excavations on Karmir-Blur yielded only carbonised pieces of cloth which had lost all their colour; there are, however, some pieces with a woven pattern of geo-metric ornament. The discoveries also included the skirt of a *kaftan* (a long tunic) made of woollen cloth with a lining of coarser material, with insets embroidered in Gobelins technique. The existence of weaving shops in Teishebaini is proved by the finding of a large number of loom weights, of a size which suggests that they were used in the weaving of coarse cloth of some width. A charred roll of such cloth was found in the excavations.

Among the animal bones discovered in considerable quantity on Karmir-Blur were whole skeletons and individual bones belonging to horses of two types, a large breed and a small one. The bronze harness-pieces and bits found by the excavators, with inscriptions in the names of Menua, Argishti and Sarduri *(Plate 79)*, belonged to the larger breed of horse, for which western Asia was famous. In a field near Van a stone was found with a cuneiform inscription saying: "Menua, son of Ishpuini, says: 'From this place the horse named Artsibi (the eagle), ridden by Menua, leapt 22 cubits.'" Clearly only a tall horse could achieve a jump of this length (about 37 feet).

In one of the store-rooms of Teishebaini containing various bronze articles was found a splendid figure of a horse's head which had once decorated the shaft of a chariot *(Plate 107)*; and bronze helmets and quivers were frequently ornamented with representations of chariots and horsemen *(Plates 85, 86, 93)*.

Thus the excavations at Karmir-Blur have enabled us to build up a vivid picture of the economy of ancient Urartu — its highly developed irrigation agriculture, its horticulture and viticulture, its stock-rearing and its craft industry. An important centre of this kind, like the leading towns of other ancient Oriental states, required to have an efficient accounting system and well organised storage facilities. The store-rooms of Teishebaini were kept securely locked, as is shown by the latch with the inscription which revealed the name of the city. For greater security, however, the doors were sealed as well as locked. The excavations brought to light a broken *bulla* from one of the large wine-cellars. This was a lump of clay mixed with bitumen in which was a knot joining two pieces of cord with which the bolt had been tied to the door. The end of each piece of cord was sealed with two different round seals — the seals of the two officials responsible for the safe keeping of the wine-cellar. A similar *bulla* found in a grain-store also bore the impressions of two seals, one round and the other cylindrical. The latter showed a tree of life between two winged animals with forequarters in human form, with a cuneiform inscription at the top and bottom saying "This is the seal of the palace of Rusa, son of Rusa."

Records and Inscriptions

The cuneiform accounting records of Teishebaini have not survived, but such records would certainly exist. Evidence of this is provided by the tablet, already referred to *(Plate 37)*, with a list of animal hides and wool, and also by two other fragments of documents. It may be noted that the only complete accounting document which has survived is inexpertly written, with a number of spelling errors.

We get an entirely different impression from the letters addressed to the viceroy at Teishebaini by the Urartian kings and high officials in the capital. They are well written, in a handsome cuneiform script, and are stamped at the end with the royal cylinder seal, which bears a representation of the tree of life with fantastic animals on either side *(Plate 34, 35, 37)*. These letters deal with the redistribution of land *(Plate 37)*, the return of a runaway slave girl *(Plate 34)*, the collection of tribute, the movement of people or animals, or problems of inheritance. They give us a picture of the daily round in the fortress, and throw light on a variety of matters which are not referred to in any other documents.

In addition to the cuneiform records on clay tablets the fortress would also possess another series of records written on papyrus, probably in Aramaic script. In the reliefs from the Assyrian palaces showing the counting up of plunder there are usually two scribes, one holding a clay tablet and a short stick, the other a scroll of papyrus and a stylus. Unfortunately our only evidence at Teishebaini of documents written on papyrus is a flat bitumen *bulla* which had been used to seal such a scroll. The obverse of this has the impression of a seal showing a man and a stag, and the reverse, which is concave, has preserved the impression of the papyrus which was consumed in the fire. Similarly, no papyrus scrolls have survived in the Assyrian palaces, and we glean our only information about a treaty between Sennacherib and the Pharaoh Shabaka from a *bulla* with two seals found, along with other seals, in a room in Sennacherib's palace in Nineveh. The documents themselves were destroyed by fire, but the clay seals survived undamaged.

We have already referred to the long inscription recording the foundation of Teishebaini which was found in 1962 on stones from the foundations of a temple in the southern part of the fortress. A second inscription — the continuation of the first — has survived only in part, only two complete blocks and a number of fragments having been found. It turned out that the fragmentary inscription found in 1936, which had led to the commencement of excavations on Karmir-Blur, fitted on to one of the blocks found in 1962. It belonged to the concluding part of the inscription, which laid a curse on anyone who should venture to destroy the building to which it related. One of the blocks forming part of the second inscription referred to the bringing of sacred weapons to be deposited at the gates of Haldi's temple. This text provides the explanation for the enormous quantity of fine bronze arms and armour which has become the special pride of Karmir-Blur. It is no exaggeration to say that the excavations have revealed a richly stocked museum of Urartian military equipment of the 8th century B.C. *(Plates 80–96)*. The finds have included a great quantity of iron and bronze weapons — arrowheads *(Plate 83)*, spears, daggers and swords *(Plate 87)*, including some long iron swords with bronze hafts. Many pieces of scale armour in iron and bronze have also been recovered; and associated with the finest piece of this armour was a button bearing an inscription in the name of Argishti I.

More than twenty quivers were found, decorated with horizontal bands of ornament depicting war chariots and horsemen *(Plates 85, 86)* and with brief dedicatory inscriptions to the god Haldi in the name of the 8th century kings Argishti I and Sarduri II. Some of the bronze arrowheads found in the quivers also had dedicatory inscriptions with the king's name.

We know that the Urartians were skilled archers; and the stone with an inscription recording the Urartian king's skill as a rider is matched by another stone, also found in a field, with an inscription commemorating Argishti II's feat in shooting an arrow a distance of 950 cubits (over 500 yards). ("Argishti, son of Rusa, fired an arrow from this spot, in front of the grove called Gilurani, as far as the garden belonging to Ishpilini, son of Batu: 950 cubits").

Also referable to the 8th century kings were a number of pointed helmets, decorated in front with representations of sacred trees with genii in front of them, and on the temples and at the rear with representations of chariots and horsemen *(Plates 93–96)*. Round the rim of the helmets were cuneiform inscriptions. Most of the twenty or so helmets found — in varying states of preservation — had a simpler form of decoration consisting of a symbolic device — a representation, for example, of lightning — on the front of the helmet.

When the first examples of this splendid equipment, dedicated to Haldi, were found it was difficult to account for the fact that most of these objects, discovered in a fortress of the 7th century B.C., dated from the 8th century. The explanation proposed was that they had been transferred from some earlier centre; and this was confirmed, though only in the final stages of the excavations, by the finding of the inscription from the foundations of a temple referring to the bringing of sacred weapons to Haldi on the occasion of the building of the fortress. The question was finally put beyond doubt by the inscriptions on the bronze shields, which were of greater length than those on other objects. Altogether seventeen shields were found, five of them being decorated with figures of bulls and lions in concentric circles *(Plates 88–92)*. The inscriptions indicated that they dated from the reigns of Argishti I, Sarduri II and Rusa I. The inscriptions on the shields bearing the name of Argishti I, the founder of the first Urartian establishment in Transcaucasia, showed that the shields had been made for the city of Erebuni, which was discussed in an earlier chapter. Thus the building of Teishebaini took place at a time when the older centre had lost its earlier importance. The name of Erebuni is also mentioned on a massive round bronze pedestal found at Teishebaini, with an inscription recording that "this wooden article" was made "when the town of Erebuni was built". The pedestal

101, 102

103, 104

no doubt belonged to a wooden statuette of a king or god, made in honour of the foundation of the town.

Statuettes of this kind were in fact found in Teishebaini — one female and four male figures, about 8 inches high, carved from wood with bronze details *(Plate 128)* (a crown, a belt, a sword, a quiver and arrows, a spearhead and — in the case of the female figure — a mirror and a large fan). These figures, representing Urartian divinities, were found in a badly damaged condition among the charred remains of branches *(Plates 127, 128)*. When first discovered they still showed traces of painting, though this later faded.

Other Finds

These statuettes of warrior gods have supplemented our information about the dress and military equipment of the Urartians. Some bronze belts were also found, decorated with geometric patterns or with figures of the three principal Urartian gods — Haldi, Teisheba and Shivini *(Plate 80)*.

As already noted, some fragments of woollen clothing were found by the excavators, but it was scarcely to be expected that any remains of footwear would have survived. Here the pottery came to the archaeologists' aid. The fine pieces found at Teishebaini included two cups in the form of boots — tall leather boots, with the lacing indicated by painted or impressed decoration *(Plates 47, 48)*. The painted cup represented a boot with a flared top; the other, of dark polished ware, was a beautifully made soft-soled boot, with the seams so meticulously rendered in the decoration that a contemporary shoemaker would have no difficulty in producing an exact copy of this specimen of Urartian footwear.

In this rapid survey of the results of the Karmir-Blur excavations it is not possible even to mention all the remarkable and interesting objects which came to light in the ruins of the citadel. The pottery was of high quality and great variety. The commonest type was polished red ware *(Plates 46, 49–54, 56, 58, 63, 64, 68);* more rarely, pieces of black pottery were found. One item of particular interest was a large black vessel with a band of painted decoration round its widest part and with three sculptured bulls' heads, similar to those found on the rim of vessels made of bronze *(Plate 55).* Considerable numbers of bronze vessels were discovered, particularly wine-cups of various types, as commonly found throughout western Asia *(Plates 97, 98).* The centrepiece of the room devoted to material from Teishebaini in the Historical Museum of Armenia in Erevan is a huge brass sacrificial cauldron with a bronze rim *(Plate 70),* similar to the cauldrons shown in front of the Musasir temple on the relief from Sargon's palace.

An outstanding example of the bronze sculpture of Teishebaini is a figurine, probably representing the god Teisheba, which originally decorated the top of a military standard *(Plate 106).* The worn condition of the figurine indicates that it had frequently been burnished to a high polish – showing evidence of a practice common to soldiers of all ages.

Much jewellery was also found, made of bronze (fibulas and small ornaments), silver (medallions with figures of gods) *(Plates 122, 123),* or gold (bracelets, ear-rings and other ornaments) *(Plates 118–121, 124).* The larger pieces include two outstanding specimens: a silver torque or neck ornament with gold figures of lions at the ends, and a silver lid with applied bands of gold and a gold pomegranate on top, bearing an inscription in the name of Argishti I.

The Urartians were also skilled in the carving of stone and bone *(Plates 115–117).* Stone beads are found in great variety, including some magnificent round and cylindrical beads of sardonyx and cornelian *(Plate 113).* Sometimes seals of various types *(Plate 40, 41)* are included in strings of beads: they may be conical in shape, or bell-shaped, or cylindrical with a suspension lug, or of the ordinary cylindrical shape with a longitudinal aperture which is common throughout western Asia. In addition to their practical use these seals also served as amulets.

Three silver medallions were also found on Karmir-Blur, one with a representation of a sacrifice to Haldi *(Plate 123)*, another with a figure of the goddess Arubani *(Plate 123)*, and the third with the symbol of the god Shivini (a winged solar disc). An interesting feature is that on the medallions with the figures of Haldi and his spouse the heads of the two divinities are on a small round gold disc soldered on to the medallion. Figures of the three principal Urartian gods were also found on bronze belts; and near a sacrificial altar in a wine-store were discovered some clay figurines of fish divinities, similar to the corresponding Assyrian deities and to figures found in the Urartian fortress at Adılcevaz. In another store-room was a painted pottery statuette of a scorpion god *(Plate 65)*. No doubt these figurines were intended to protect the contents of the store-rooms from evil spirits.

Influences and Connections

Many objects were found in Teishebaini showing connections between the Urartian centres in Transcaucasia and the civilisations of the ancient East. Among such items were some magnificent examples of Assyrian cylinder seals *(Plates 39, 43)*, including a cornelian seal of the period of the Sargonids with a figure of a king hunting wild bulls from a chariot. Many faience seals *(Plate 45)* and beads found at Karmir-Blur have direct analogies with material recovered during the excavation of the Assyrian capital city of Assur. There are also bronze cups and beads of Assyrian origin.

Teishebaini's links with the countries of Asia Minor and the Mediterranean are demonstrated by a silver jug with a palmette under the handle and a hieroglyphic inscription *(Plates 71–73)* similar to that on one of the bronze wine-cups, and by a pair of padlock-shaped earrings with granulated decoration *(Plate 119)*. The geometric decoration on a white background which is found on a vessel of *askos* type *(Plate 58)* is probably to be related to a type of decoration used in Asia Minor. A fragment of a glazed faience vessel with a seated female figure has its closest analogies on the island of Rhodes *(Plate 61)*. A faience amulet statuette of the goddess Sohmet and some scaraboid objects with Egyptian hieroglyphs *(Plate 44)* may have come from Egypt or northern Syria. And a detailed study of the stone beads would undoubtedly reveal further evidence of the wide-ranging connections between the Urartian cities and the countries of the ancient East.

The store-rooms of Teishebaini also contained Scythian objects, coming not only from the Scythians of the northern Caucasus but also from those of the Dnieper area. Among the items in the latter group is an iron bit with curb-rings formed of discs of bone decorated with the head of an animal — a sheep or a horse (on the examples found at Karmir-Blur the head is missing) — on the upper part and a hoof on the lower part. Also of Scythian origin are some hemispherical faience beads decorated with grooves and horn belt-buckles in the shape of sheep's heads, of a type familiar from the Kelermes *kurgans*. Alongside the flat Urartian arrowheads, either of bronze or iron, with a long tang for securing them to the shaft, considerable numbers of bipennate and trilobate bronze arrowheads of Scythian type were found in the Teishebaini store-rooms.

It is not open to doubt, therefore, that the Scythians maintained close connections with this Transcaucasian outpost of Urartu, and through it with the other countries of the ancient East. It is possible, indeed, that some objects of Scythian type were made in Teishebaini itself. At the main (south) gate of the citadel was a gate-keeper's lodge which, like the rest of the fortress, had been destroyed in the final conflagration. The excavations showed that the door-keeper had occupied himself with working in horn, for in his house were found sawn-up pieces of stagshorn ready for carving and the head of a griffin in the Scythian style. The griffin's head showed signs of wear from long use, and cannot therefore have been the work of this local craftsman: very probably he was using it as a model.

The Urartian objects found in Teishebaini, particularly the bronze belts *(Plate 80)* which are also met with in other areas in Transcaucasia, show many decorative elements — such as, for example, the representations of sacred trees in characteristically stylised form — which form a link between some of the objects in the Ziwiye treasure and certain works of Scythian art such as the gold facings of dagger sheaths from the Kelermes and Melgunov *kurgans*. It is now no longer possible to study the relationships between the Scythians and the various countries of the ancient East without taking account of the Karmir-Blur material.

Layout of the Town

As we have already noted, round the citadel of Teishebaini, covering an area of between 75 and 100 acres, lay the city. It was surrounded by a wall, but the defences apparently remained unfinished: it may be, indeed, that the town itself was never completed according to plan.

The architecture of the town makes it clear that the population covered a range of different ranks and social classes. There are blocks of identical dwellings entered from an open courtyard, with no store-rooms, occupied by families whose subsistence was provided for by the state; and there are other houses which seem to have been the private dwellings of the more prosperous citizens, each containing several rooms as well as storage accommodation for provisions. Still another type of building, discovered in 1961, is of particular interest. It had a total area of nearly 20,000 square feet and consisted of four eleven-roomed dwellings of identical plan. There were four entrances in one of the walls, which in external appearance resembled a three-storey building represented on a bronze plaque found at Toprak-kale. It is quite likely that the building excavated at Teishebaini was two-storied.

The regular layout of the town and the types of houses — the blocks of small flats and the building containing larger houses — suggest that the whole town was built in advance for occupation by people transferred here from other areas.

Like Erebuni, the town would certainly be built with the labour of prisoners of war and the local population. It was inhabited by the craftsmen who worked in the various workshops in the fortress, agricultural workers, soldiers of the Urartian garrison and a variety of officials — the typical population of an ancient Oriental city, a centre of administration and of economic life.

The Destruction of Teishebaini

The excavations at Teishebaini have yielded a vivid picture of the fall of the city at the beginning of the 6th century B.C. (about 590–585), when the kingdom of Urartu was tottering in the face of attack by the Medes. The citadel was destroyed and set on fire in a night attack directed not against the well defended main gate but against the postern gate in the north-west corner. Before the final assault the citadel came under heavy fire from the enemy archers; and numbers of bronze arrows of the Scythian trilobate type were extracted from the adobe brick of the walls near the postern. It is clear that the attackers of the Urartian fortress included some of their former allies, the Scythians.

The city was abandoned on the approach of the enemy, and the defenders of Teishebaini entrenched themselves in the citadel, fitting up temporary living accommodation in the courtyard and the fortress buildings and laying in large stores of provisions. The attack took place in July or August: the harvest had been gathered, but the grapes were still ripening and the wine jars stood empty and unstoppered in the great store-rooms. In one of the jars were found traces of sulphur: evidently they were being fumigated to disinfect them. Mice and hamsters had found their way into the open jars, as was shown by the skeletons found by the excavators; in one jar were the remains of a cat. The time of year when the fortress was destroyed was also indicated by the dried grass of a broom which had been used to sweep the floor of one of the store-rooms. In the charred fragments botanists were able to distinguish the almost invisible remains of flowers, and these also pointed to the end of summer.

Before the assault the remaining population who had taken refuge in the citadel removed their possessions from the store-rooms, divided them out and concealed them as best they could, sometimes covering them with branches or with grain, sometimes burying them in the earth floor. These caches of property show evidence of the sharing-out process. They may contain, for example, a single gold ear-ring *(Plate 119)*, or one half of a silver neck ornament decorated with a gold lion at one end *(Plate 120)*, or half of a bronze cauldron, or detached pieces from a set of harness. In some of the caches were found clay tablets with seal impressions representing a sacred tree.

No doubt the defenders of the fortress expected to be able to recover these articles after the siege had been beaten off; and perhaps with this in mind the hiding-place of a shield and a sword buried in the floor was marked by a cross drawn on the wall in brown paint. Fate, however, decided otherwise. The fortress was taken in a night assault and burned to the ground. The makeshift dwellings in the courtyard of the citadel caught fire, and their whole contents were buried when the roof of timber and brushwood crashed down in flames. The occupants had barely time to escape as their houses collapsed: a man's weapons were left abandoned by the hearth, a woman's ornaments fell unnoticed in a corner. Under the debris were found the skeletons of a child and of an ass (which had presumably been tethered). All this pointed to a sudden night attack. The citadel itself was destroyed in the conflagration, and the roofs and walls of the upper floor collapsed, burying in their fall anything that was not completely consumed. In the recesses of the store-rooms in the north-eastern part of the citadel were found the half-burned skeletons of people who had vainly been seeking safety; among the remains was a gold bracelet which one of them had presumably been carrying concealed about his person. The half-consumed skull of one man who had fallen on the earth floor contained the carbonised remains of the brain *(Plate 28)*.

But the fire did not destroy everything. Clay objects like the tablets from the official archives were hardened by the heat, and many materials — cloth, yarn, grass — were preserved by carbonisation. One remarkable find was a pomegranate flower in which the stamens and pistils as well as the sepals had survived, though the petals had fallen off. The flower was reinforced with synthetic resins and is now preserved — a fragile glass bloom — in the Armenian Museum of Winemaking.

After the fall of Teishebaini life never returned to the city, and the hill of Karmir-Blur and the whole city area long remained empty and desolate. Meanwhile other Urartian centres like Erebuni which had been abandoned earlier, but where life did not come to an end, continued to exist; and excavations on these sites have revealed well-preserved remains of structures of the 6th to the 4th centuries B.C. incorporating older Urartian buildings with cuneiform inscriptions in the name of Urartian kings of the 8th century B.C.

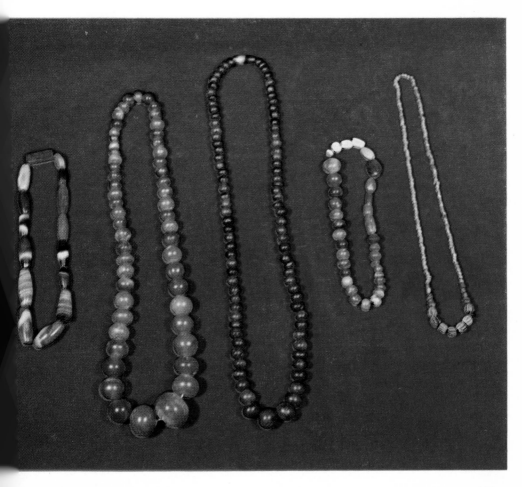

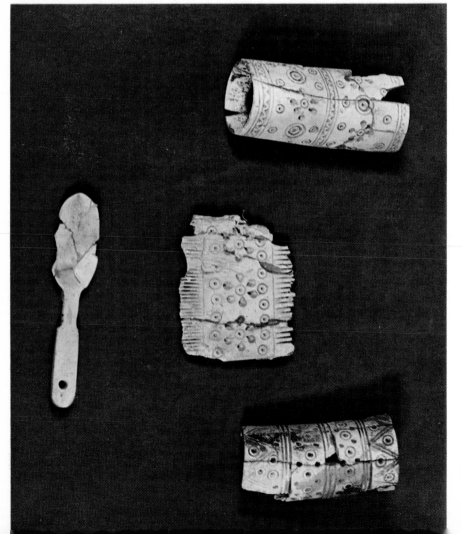

114, 11

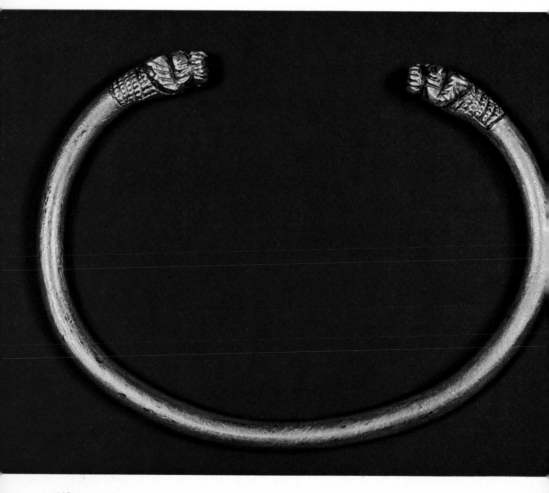

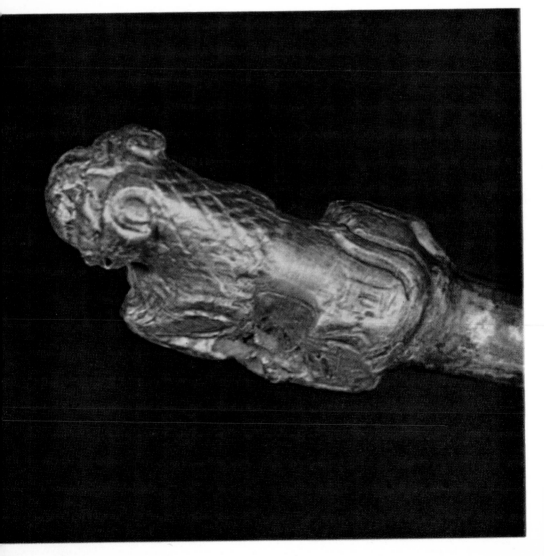

122, 123

124, 125

126

127

128

Conclusion

As the discussion in earlier chapters has indicated, our knowledge of Urartian history is based on three parallel sources — Assyrian annals and works of art, Urartian inscriptions, and the material obtained by the excavation of Urartian fortresses and cemeteries.

The information provided by these three different sources is complementary. Our knowledge of the formation of the Urartian kingdom and its history during the 9th century B.C. comes solely from the Assyrian written sources, which give us a chronological framework: indeed the whole chronology of the Urartian kings depends on dated references to them in the Assyrian annals.

The events of the 8th century B.C. are recorded in both Assyrian and Urartian texts, but the two sources give different information, complementing rather than duplicating one another. The reason for this is clear enough: the Assyrians recount their victories and say nothing of their defeats, and the Urartians follow an exactly similar policy. Thus the Assyrian and Urartian annals never contain precisely the same facts.

Archaeological investigation of 8th century sites is only beginning, and the sites which have received most attention are the Urartian fortresses of the 7th century B.C., the period when the Assyrian and Urartian written sources begin to fail us. In this period the historians have nothing to go on but the brief accounts given in foundation inscriptions and a few laconic references to kings' names; and the study of Urartian history and culture in this second period now rests, therefore, in the hands of the archaeologists.

The excavations at Teishebaini (Karmir-Blur) have yielded a vivid picture of Urartian culture throughout almost the whole course of the 7th century B.C., and have also given us much information about Urartian art of the 8th century through the discovery of material transferred from earlier Urartian settlements.

EPILOGUE

V

The Last Kings of Urartu

When Teishebaini fell the whole Urartian kingdom was in process of collapse. The same fate befell Rusahinili (Toprakkale), the residence of the Urartian kings in their capital of Tushpa. The Toprakkale excavations have shown that this town also was destroyed and given over to the flames, and in addition have yielded many bronze shields from the walls of the temple with inscriptions in the name of one of the last Urartian kings — Rusa, son of Erimena, whose name also appears in a brief inscription recording the construction of a granary found at Argishtihinili in Transcaucasia.

The Teishebaini excavations brought to light many inscriptions mentioning the names of Urartian kings. The life of this city coincides exactly with the second period in the history of the Kingdom of Van: the fortress was built in the reign of Rusa II, during the resurgence of Urartu, and its massive strength bears witness to the might of the Urartian kingdom.

When he built this new fortress Rusa II recorded his achievements on the walls of the main temple, deposited in it treasure brought from other Urartian fortresses, and adorned the temples with ornamental shields bearing inscriptions in the name of his predecessors. The inscriptions of Rusa II are the last Urartian lapidary inscriptions known to us: for the later period we have only cuneiform documents on clay tablets and brief texts inscribed on bronze objects. This period, however, was of considerable length. The last occurrence of Rusa II's name in the Assyrian annals of Ashurbanipal's reign is in connection with events in the year 654 B.C., and his son Sarduri III is recorded as coming to Assyria in the year 639: we may conclude, therefore, that between Rusa II's death and the fall of Urartu in 590–585 B.C. there elapsed a period of some sixty years. During this period the Urartian throne was occupied by five kings, of whom nothing is known beyond their names.

Although Sarduri III, son of Rusa II, sent greetings and gifts to the Assyrian King Ashurbanipal he evidently also maintained good relations with the Scythians. It is he who is referred to in the following words from a hymn to the god Ashur written by Ashurbanipal himself: "The Urartians also, that proud mountain people, carry on intrigues with the Umman-Manda (the nomads), the perfidious foe, and are constantly committing great abominations against thee." Two tablets found in Teishebaini contained orders from Sarduri III about the redistribution of land and the delivery of animals.

After the time of Sarduri III the Assyrian written sources contain no references to any Urartian king, and the Urartian inscriptions mention the names of kings only on votive objects and in brief texts on seals. Even these laconic references, however, reveal one or two unexpected facts. A seal impression on one of the Karmir-Blur tablets mentions the name of "Sarduri, son of Sarduri", who might have been supposed to be a prince of the royal house, since on succeeding to the throne a king never bore the same name as his father, and since a tablet containing an intelligence report found at Teishebaini is sealed with "the prince's seal". Then the excavators discovered a bronze shield with an inscription on the rim which departed from the usual stereotype and referred to Sarduri, son of Sarduri, as king. No doubt at this period it had become necessary to replace some of the shields which hung on the walls of the temple, or to add new ones, and Rusa II's grandson had inscribed his name on the new shields.

A similar renewal of the temple ornaments in the city of Rusahinili (Toprakkale) was carried out by Rusa III, son of Erimena, whose father's name is preserved only in a seal impression on a document found at Teishebaini *(Plate 35)*. The shields found at Toprakkale with inscriptions in the name of Rusa III are of high artistic quality, and the inscriptions repeat the dedicatory formulae used on the shields presented by his predecessors. It is usually thought that Rusa, son of Erimena, was the last Urartian king, whose reign — hitherto prosperous — was interruped by a Median invasion about the year 585 B.C., when the Median forces passed through the Urartian capital on their way to meet the army of the Lydian King Alyattes on the River Halys. Here again, however, the epigraphical material from Karmir-Blur yields fresh evidence. On two different seal impressions, one on a clay tablet and the other on a *bulla* sealing the door of a granary, the name "Rusa, son of Rusa" can be read. In brief inscriptions of this kind the royal title is omitted, and we cannot, therefore, be sure that Rusa IV was king and not merely a prince — though the former possibility is entirely plausible. It would thus appear that the ruthless destruction of Rusahinili in central Urartu and of Teishebaini on the periphery of the kingdom took place in the reign of Rusa IV, and the sequence of kings in the second period of Urartian history would then be: Rusa II — Sarduri III — Sarduri IV — Erimena — Rusa III — Rusa IV.

The Decline of Assyria and the Rise of the Scythians

After Rusa II the kingdom of Urartu ceased to be of any importance in the history of western Asia, though it still contrived to outlast its great enemy Assyria. In the second half of the 7th century B.C. Assyria began to lose its power and its possessions, being involved in bitter conflict with Babylonia, which had rebelled against its authority, and with the rising power of Media. An alliance with Egypt did not avail to save Assyria, and in 614 B.C. the Medes captured and destroyed Assur, and Cyaxares the Mede and King Nabupalasar of Babylonia concluded an alliance amid the ruins. In 612 B.C., after a long siege by the Babylonians and Medes, Nineveh fell. In the final attack, as Herodotus tells us, a decisive part was played by the arrival of a large Scythian army led by Madyes, son of Protothyes (the Partatua of the Assyrian sources). The last Assyrian king, Ashur-uballit, was compelled to withdraw to Harran, where he managed to hold out until 610 B.C.; then in the year 605, after the fall of Carchemish, the Assyrian kingdom ceased to exist.

The part played by the Scythians and other nomadic tribes in the destruction of Assyria and other ancient Oriental kingdoms is again documented by archaeological material. In many parts of western Asia tanged arrowheads have been found, bilobate or trilobate in shape, distinct from the normal western Asian type and similar to the Scythian type. These arrowheads may also have belonged to the Medes, since the Median army had equipment similar to that of the Scythians and the Medes, like the Scythians, were famed for their skill in archery. Many arrows of Scythian type have also been picked up on the sites of ancient battles in which the Medes took part. Arrows of this kind were found, for example, at Assur, Nineveh and Kalhu, sometimes in circumstances which made it quite clear that they had been fired by enemy hands.

A Babylonian chronicle which gives us a detailed account, month by month, of events between 616 and 609 B.C., mainly connected with the defeat of Assyria, refers to an expedition against Urartu (and specifically against the town of Urashtu) in the year 609; but the outcome of the campaign is not known, since the text breaks off at this point.

In a continuation of this text, written on another tablet and giving an account of events from 608 to 605 B.C., there is a further reference to an expedition by Nabupalasar into the mountainous area of Bit-Hanunia, "a district in the land of Urartu". It is possible that these expeditions by the Babylonians against Urartu were confined to the frontier areas. At any rate the kingdom of Urartu was still in existence at the beginning of the 6th century B.C., and a passage in the Book of *Jeremiah* dated to the fourth year of the reign of King Zedekiah (i.e., 594 B.C.) talks of calling together against Babylon the Medes, the Urartians ("Ararat"), the Mannaeans ("Minni") and the Scythians ("Ashchenaz"). It is noteworthy that the Scythians are now referred to in association with other nations of western Asia. Excavations in Iran have revealed, in the Ziwiye treasure, an important collection of material belonging to the Scythians of western Asia, reflecting a syncretic art style

198

in which both ancient Oriental and Scythian elements are clearly evident. In the same burials were found Assyrian articles of the mid-8th century B.C., captured by the Scythians when they destroyed the Assyrian cities.

The Urartian kingdom ceased to exist at the beginning of the 6th century B.C. The arrowheads found in the adobe walls of Teishebaini indicate that the Scythians — the Urartians' erstwhile allies — took part in the destruction of the northern Urartian centres and helped the Transcaucasian tribes to throw off the heavy Urartian yoke.

The Urartian objects found in burials in the mountainous areas of the Caucasus evidently come from the plundered Urartian settlements of the southern Caucasus, in particular from Teishebaini. Thus an Urartian belt with representations of war chariots, lions and bulls was found in a cemetery at the village of Tli in southern Osetia, and a similar belt was found in a burial excavated at Zeyva in Armenia. Many years ago a bronze helmet, now in the Berlin Museum, was found in an ancient cemetery at Verkhnaya Rutkha in northern Osetia, but only within the last few years has it been noticed that on the front of the helmet is a symbolic device of the same type as on the helmets found at Karmir-Blur; and subsequent restoration work has revealed an inscription in the name of Argishti I. The helmet may have been a trophy taken at the destruction of Teishebaini.

After the fall of Urartu its place was taken by new kingdoms and new groupings of the countries which had formed part of the Urartian kingdom. Thus on the western periphery of Urartian territory there grew up an alliance of tribes headed by the Armenians. (We have already noted that a country known as Arme, lying to the south-west of Lake Van, is referred to in the annals as early as the reign of Sarduri II.)

The region round Lake Van, the ancient nucleus of Urartu, became at first a Median possession and later, for many years, formed part of Achaemenid Persia. The city of Rusahinili (Toprakkale) was now a burnt-out ruin, and the old fortress on the crag of Van therefore took on a fresh lease of life, as is shown by a foundation inscription recording building work carried out by Xerxes.

In the southern Caucasus the ruins of Teishebaini remained abandoned and desolate, but life continued in the old settlement of Erebuni, where excavation has revealed buildings of the Achaemenid period.

We know from Achaemenid cuneiform inscriptions that in the middle of the 6th century B.C. a considerable area of Urartian territory was occupied by the Armenians. In the list of countries conquered by Darius (c. 520 B.C.), as recorded in the Babylonian texts of the Naqsh-i Rustam and Behistun inscriptions, we still find the ancient designation of Urartu, in the Babylonian form Urashtu; but in the Old Persian and Elamite texts this is replaced by the term Armina. Thus the area which had been the Kingdom of Van was beginning to be called by the name of the new political grouping which had taken over a large part of its territory.

The name of Urartu is mentioned for the last time in a document of the time of Darius II (c. 415 B.C.), but by this time it undoubtedly meant the land of Armina.

Historians have been much exercised by the fate of the Urartians after the fall of the kingdom of Urartu. It was long thought that, under pressure from the Armenians, they had abandoned their country and withdrawn northward. The view now generally accepted, however, is that they remained where they were and mingled with the Armenians. The resemblance between the dress of the Armenians, as shown in the reliefs from Xerxes' palace in Persepolis, and that of the Urartian emissaries in a relief from Ashurbanipal's palace in Nineveh has long been recognised. The reason is not far to seek; for the Armenians who took over the territory of the ancient kingdom of Urartu likewise assimilated its culture.

CHRONOLOGICAL TABLE

Assyria	Dates	Urartu
Shalmaneser III (860–825)	860 858 846 834	Aramu Sarduri I
Shamshi-Adad (825–812)	824	Ishpuini, son of Sarduri
Queen Sammuramat (812–803)		
Adad-nirarí III (812–783)		Menua, son of Ishpuini
Shalmaneser IV (783–773)		
Ashur-dan III (773–754)		Argishti, son of Menua
Ashur-nirari IV (754–745)		Sarduri, son of Argishti
Tiglath-Pileser III (745–727)	743 735	
Shalmaneser V (727–722)		Rusa, son of Sarduri (714+)
Sargon (722–705)	714	
Sennacherib (705–681)		Argishti, son of Rusa
Esarhaddon (681–668)		Rusa, son of Argishti
Ashurbanipal (668–624)	654 639	Sarduri, son of Rusa (Sarduri, son of Sarduri?)
Fall of Nineveh (612)		Erimena
		Rusa, son of Erimena
		(Rusa, son of Rusa?)
		(Fall of Urartu, c. 585)

Note: The dates in the middle column are the dates of references in the Assyrian annals to kings of Urartu.

BIBLIOGRAPHY

General Works

E. AKURGAL, "Urartäische Kunst", *Anatolia*, IV, 1959, p. 77.

N.V. ARUTYUNYAN, *Zemledelie i skotovodstvo v Urartu* ("Agriculture and Stock-Rearing in Urartu"), Erevan, 1964.

A. GOETZE, *Kleinasien* (Müller, *Handbuch der Altertumswissenschaft*, III, 1, iii), 2nd ed., Munich, 1957.

C.F. LEHMANN-HAUPT, *Armenien einst und jetzt*, I-III, 1910–22.

G.A. MELIKISHVILI, *Nairi-Urartu*, Tbilisi, 1954.

B.B. PIOTROVSKY, *Istoriya i kultura Urartu* ("The History and Culture of Urartu"), Erevan, 1944.

B.B. PIOTROVSKY, *Vanskoe tsarstvo* ("The Kingdom of Van"), Moscow, 1959

M. RIEMENSCHNEIDER, *Das Reich am Ararat*, Leipzig, 1965.

Urartian Culture; Excavations

P. AMANDRY, "Objets orientaux en Grèce et en Italie aux VIIIe et VIIe siècles avant J.-Chr.", *Syria*, XXXV, 1958, p. 73.

R.D. BARNETT, "The Excavations of the British Museum at Toprak Kale near Van", *Iraq*, XII, 1950, p. 1.

R.D. BARNETT, N. GÖKÇE, "The Find of Urartian Bronzes at Altın Tepe near Erzincan", *Anatolian Studies*, III, 1953, p. 111.

E. BILGIÇ, B. ÖĞÜN, "Excavations at Kef Kalesi of Adılcevaz, 1964", Anatolia, VIII, 1964, p. 93.

M. BROSSET, "Etudes sur les monuments géorgiens photographiés par M. Jermakof", *Bulletin of the Imperial Academy of St Petersburg*, XVI, 1871, p. 433.

C.A. BURNEY, "Urartian Fortresses and Towns in the Van Region", *Anatolian Studies*, VII, 1957, p. 37.

A. ERZEN, "Untersuchungen in der urartäischen Stadt Toprakkale bei Van in den Jahren 1959–61", *Archäologischer Anzeiger (1962)*, 1963, p. 383.

R.W. HAMILTON, "The Decorated Bronze Strip from Gushchi", *Anatolian Studies*, XV, 1965, p. 41.

K. HOFFMANN, J. FRIEDRICH, "Der urartäische Kandelaber in Hamburg und seine Keilinschrift", *Zeitschrift der Deutschen Morgenländischen Gesellschaft*, N.F. 36, 1961, p. 283.

C.F. LEHMANN-HAUPT, "Materialien zur älteren Geschichte Armeniens und Mesopotamiens", *Abhandlungen der Königlichen Gesellschaft der Wissenschaften zu Göttingen, Phil.-hist. Klasse*, IX, 3, 1906, p 65.

I.M. LOSEVA, S.I. KHODZHASH, "Desyat let rabot po raskopkam urartskogo goroda Erebuni" ("Ten years' work on the excavation of the Urartian town of Erebuni"), *Publications of the Pushkin Museum, Moscow*, II, 1964.

N.Y. MARR, I.A. ORBELI, *Arkheologicheskaya ekspeditsiya 1916 g. v Van* ("The 1916 Archaeological Expedition to Van"), Petrograd, 1922.

K.R. MAXWELL-HYSLOP, "Urartian Bronzes in Etruscan Tombs", *Iraq*, XVIII, 1956, p. 150.

M.J. MELLINK, "Archaeology in Asia Minor", *American Journal of Archaeology*, 64, 1960, p. 64; 65, 1961, p. 43; 66, 1962, p. 76; 67, 1963, p. 181; 68, 1964, p. 158; 69, 1965, p. 141; 70, 1966, p. 149.

G.R. MEYER, "Ein neuentdeckter urartäischer Brustschmuck", *Das Altertum*, I, 1955, p. 205.

K.L. OGANESYAN, *Arin-berd I: Arkhitektura Erebuni* ("Arin-Berd I: the Architecture of Erebuni"), Erevan, 1961.

K.L. OGANESYAN, *Karmir-blur IV: Arkhitektura Teishebaini* ("Karmir-Blur IV: the Architecture of Teishebaini"), Erevan, 1955.

B. ÖĞÜN, "Kurze Geschichte der Ausgrabungen in Van und die türkischen Versuchsgrabungen auf dem Toprak-kale 1959", *Zeitschrift der Deutschen Morgenländischen Gesellschaft*, N.F. 36, 1961, p. 254.

T. ÖZGÜÇ, *Altıntepe*, Ankara, 1966.

T. ÖZGÜÇ, "Excavations at Altıntepe", *Türk Tarih Kurumu Belleten*, XXV, 1961.

T. ÖZGÜÇ, "The Urartian Architecture on the Summit of Altıntepe", *Anatolia*, VII, 1963, p. 43.

M. PALLOTTINO, "Urartu, Greece and Etruria", *East and West* (Rome), IX, 1959, p. 29.

B.B. PIOTROVSKY, *Iskusstvo Urartu* ("The Art of Urartu"), Leningrad, 1962.

B.B. PIOTROVSKY, *Karmir-blur: Resultaty raskopok* ("Karmir-Blur: Results of the Excavations"), I-III, Erevan, 1950, 1952, 1955.

F.E. SCHULZ, "Mémoires sur le lac de Van et ses environs", *Journal Asiatique*, IX, 1940, p. 257.

Urartian Inscriptions

N.V. ARUTYUNYAN, *Novye urartskie nadpisi Karmir-blura* ("New Urartian Inscriptions from Karmir-Blur"), Erevan, 1966.

K. BALKAN, "Ein urartäischer Tempel auf Anzavurtepe bei Patnos und hier entdeckte Inschriften", *Anatolia*, V. 1960, p. 99.

T. BERAN, "Zur Inschrift Sardurs III bei Jzoli", *Istanbuler Mitteilungen*, VII, 1957, p. 133.

I.M. DYAKONOV, *Urartskie pisma i dokumenty* ("Urartian Letters and Documents"), Moscow and Leningrad, 1963.

J. FRIEDRICH, "Neue urartäische Inschriften", *Zeitschrift der Deutschen Morgenländischen Gesellschaft*, N.F. 30, 1955, p. 53.

P. HULIN, "Urartian Stones in the Van Museum", *Anatolian Studies*, VIII, 1958, p. 235.

P. HULIN, "New Urartian Inscriptions from Adılcevaz", *Anatolian Studies*, IX, 1959, p. 189.

F.W. KÖNIG, *Handbuch der chaldischen Inschriften*, I, II, Graz, 1955–57.

C.F. LEHMANN-HAUPT, *Corpus Inscriptionum Chaldicarum*, I, 1928; II, 1935.

G.A. MELIKISHVILI, *Urartskie klinoobraznye nadpisi* ("Urartian Cuneiform Inscriptions"), Moscow, 1960.

M.V. NIKOLSKY, "Klinoobraznye nadpisi Zakavkazya" ("Cuneiform inscriptions of Transcaucasia"), *Papers on the Archaeology of the Caucasus*, V, Moscow, 1896.

A.H. SAYCE, "The Cuneiform Inscriptions of Van", *Journal of the Royal Asiatic Society*, XIV, 1882, p. 377.

The Assyrian Sources

A. BILLERBECK, F. DELITZSCH, "Die Palasttore Salmanassars II von Balawat", *Beiträge zur Assyriologie*, VI, 1, 1908.

P.E. BOTTA, E. FLANDIN, *Monuments de Ninive*, Paris, 1849–50, II, Plates 139–147.

C.J. GADD, *The Fall of Nineveh*, London and Oxford, 1923.

I.M. DYAKONOV, "Assiro-vavilonskie istochniki po istorii Urartu" ("Assyro-Babylonian sources on the history of Urartu"), *Vestnik drevney istorii*, 1951, 2 and 3 (Supplement).

E. EBELING, B. MEISSNER, E. WEIDNER, *Die Inschriften der Altassyrischen Könige*, Leipzig, 1926, p. 113.

E.G. KLAUBER, *Politisch-religiöse Texte aus der Sargonidenzeit*, Leipzig, 1931.

J.A. KNUDTZON, *Assyrische Gebete an den Sonnengott*, II, Leipzig, 1893.

B. MEISSNER, "Die Eroberung der Stadt Ulhu auf Sargons 8. Feldzug", *Zeitschrift für Assyriologie*, XXXIV, 1922, p. 105.

A.T.E. OLMSTEAD, *Western Asia in the Days of Sargon of Assyria*, New York, 1918.

O. SCHROEDER, *Keilschrifttexte aus Assur historischen Inhalts*, II, Leipzig, 1921

M. STRECK, *Assurbanipal und die letzten assyrischen Könige*, I, Leipzig, 1916, p. 376.

E. THUREAU-DANGIN, *Une Relation de la Huitième Campagne de Sargon,* Paris, 1912.

L. WATERMAN, "Royal Correspondence of the Assyrian Empire", *University of Michigan Studies*, XVII-XX, 1930–36.

H. WINCKLER, *Die Keilschrifttexte Sargons I*, Leipzig, 1899.

LIST OF ILLUSTRATIONS

1 *Arin-Berd (Erebuni). General view of the excavations. 8th century B.C.*

2 *Arin-Berd (Erebuni). General view of the excavations. 8th century B.C.*

3 *Arin-Berd (Erebuni). Excavations in the palace. 8th century B.C.*

4 *Arin-Berd (Erebuni). Excavations in the palace. 8th century B.C.*

5 *Arin-Berd (Erebuni). A room in the palace. 8th century B.C.*

6 *Arin-Berd (Erebuni). General view of the* susi *temple. 8th century B.C.*

7 *Arin-Berd (Erebuni). Rooms with column bases. 8th century B.C.*

8 *Fragment of wall painting discovered by K. L. Oganesyan. Winged genius beside the sacred tree. Arin-Berd (Erebuni). 8th century B.C. Armenian Historical Museum, Erevan.*

9 *Fragment of wall painting depicting a bull. Arin-Berd (Erebuni). 8th century B.C. Armenian Historical Museum, Erevan.*

10 *Fragment of wall painting. Genius beside the sacred tree. Arin-Berd (Erebuni). 8th century B.C. Armenian Historical Museum, Erevan.*

11 *Wall painting, partly restored. Arin-Berd (Erebuni). Armenian Historical Museum, Erevan.*

12 *Wall painting, partly restored. Arin-Berd (Erebuni). Armenian Historical Museum, Erevan.*

13 *Wall painting, partly restored, depicting the god Haldi. Arin-Berd (Erebuni). 8th century B.C. Armenian Historical Museum, Erevan.*

14 *Fragment of stone slab with polychrome inlays. Toprakkale. 7th century B.C. Hermitage Museum, Leningrad.*

15 *Fragment of a marble frieze depicting a bull. Toprakkale. 7th century B.C. Hermitage Museum, Leningrad.*

16 *Wall painting, largely restored. Karmir-Blur. 7th century B.C. Armenian Historical Museum, Erevan.*

17 *Karmir-Blur (Teishebaini). General view from the north; in the background, Mount Ararat. 7th century B.C.*

18 *Karmir-Blur. General view of the excavations. 7th century B.C.*

19 *Karmir-Blur. General view of the excavations in the western part of the cita-del. 7th century B.C.*

20 *Karmir-Blur. General view from the south. 7th century B.C.*

21 *Karmir-Blur. The walls of the citadel (western part). 7th century B.C.*

22 *Karmir-Blur. Inner wall of the citadel. 7th century B.C.*

23 *Karmir-Blur. Room with three buttresses. 7th century B.C.*

24 *Karmir-Blur. Buttress in one of the rooms. 7th century B.C.*

25 *Basalt quern. Karmir-Blur. 7th century B.C. Hermitage Museum, Leningrad.*

26 *Karmir-Blur. Remains of plums. 7th century B.C.*

27 *Karmir-Blur. Cow's stomach. 7th century B.C.*

28 *Karmir-Blur. Human skull and brain. 7th century B.C.*

29 *Pottery dishes containing grain. From left to right: millet, wheat, barley. Karmir-Blur. 7th century B.C. Hermitage Museum, Leningrad.*

30 *Karmir-Blur. Store-room containing oil of sesame. 7th century B.C.*

31 *Remains of an old Urartian water channel near Karmir-Blur.*

32 *Karmir-Blur. Brick wall. 7th century B.C.*

33 *Karmir-Blur. A store-room. 7th century B.C.*

34 *Clay tablet with cuneiform inscriptions and a seal impression. Order for the return of an escaped slave girl. Karmir-Blur. 7th century B.C. Armenian Historical Museum, Erevan.*

35 *Clay tablet with cuneiform inscriptions and the impression of King Erimena's seal. Karmir-Blur. 7th century B.C. Armenian Historical Museum, Erevan.*

36 *Clay tablet with cuneiform inscriptions, from the archives of a fortress. List of hides and wool. Karmir-Blur. 7th century B.C. Armenian Historical Museum, Erevan.*

37 *Clay tablet with cuneiform inscriptions and a seal impression. Royal order for the redistribution of land. Karmir-Blur. 7th century B.C. Armenian Historical Museum, Erevan.*

38 *Stone with cuneiform inscriptions recording the foundation of the fortress of Erebuni by King Argishti I. Arin-Berd. 8th century B.C. Armenian Historical Museum, Erevan.*

39 *Assyrian cylinder seals, with impressions. Pottery. Karmir-Blur. 8th century B.C. Armenian Historical Museum, Erevan.*

40 *Urartian seal, with impressions. Stone. Karmir-Blur. 8th century B.C. Armenian Historical Museum, Erevan.*

41 *Bell-shaped Urartian seals, with impressions. Stone. Karmir-Blur. 8th century B.C. Armenian Historical Museum, Erevan.*

42 *Conical Urartian seals, with impressions. Stone. Karmir-Blur. 8th century B.C. Armenian Historical Museum, Erevan.*

43 *Assyrian and Babylonian cylinder seals. Stone and pottery. Karmir-Blur. 8th century B.C. Armenian Historical Museum, Erevan.*

44 *Egyptian objects: figurine of the goddess Sohmet and scarab. 8th century B.C. Armenian Historical Museum, Erevan.*

45 *Flat Assyrian seals. Faience. Karmir-Blur. 8th century B.C. Armenian Historical Museum, Erevan.*

46 *Perfume-brazier of red pottery. Karmir-Blur. 7th century B.C. Hermitage Museum, Leningrad.*

47 *Painted cup in the form of a boot. Pottery. Karmir-Blur. 8th century B.C. Armenian Historical Museum, Erevan.*

48 *Cup in the form of a boot. Pottery. Karmir-Blur. 8th century B.C. Armenian Historical Museum, Erevan.*

49 *Jugs of red pottery. Karmir-Blur. 7th century B.C. Hermitage Museum, Leningrad.*

50 *Jug, with inscription on the handle indicating its capacity. Red pottery. Karmir-Blur. 7th century B.C. Hermitage Museum, Leningrad.*

51 *Jar of red pottery. Karmir-Blur. 8th–7th century B.C. Armenian Historical Museum, Erevan.*

52 *Double oil bottle. Pottery. Karmir-Blur. 7th century B.C. Hermitage Museum, Leningrad.*

53 *Pottery jars. Karmir-Blur. 7th century B.C. Hermitage Museum, Leningrad.*

54 *Cult vessel* (kernos). *Pottery. Karmir-Blur. 8th–7th century B.C. Armenian Historical Museum, Erevan.*

55 *Pottery cauldron. Karmir-Blur. 8th century B.C. Armenian Historical Museum, Erevan.*

56 *Corn jar, with lid. Pottery. Karmir-Blur. 7th century B.C. Hermitage Museum, Leningrad.*

57 *Fermentation jar (for the brewing of beer). Red pottery. Karmir-Blur. 7th century B.C. Hermitage Museum, Leningrad.*

58 Askos-*type jug. Painted pottery. Karmir-Blur. 8th century B.C. Armenian Historical Museum, Erevan.*

59 *Large pottery jug. From excavations by A. Martirosyan. Armavir (Argishtihinili). 8th century B.C. Armenian Historical Museum, Erevan.*

60 *Fragment of a jug representing a woman. Faience. Karmir-Blur. 8th century B.C. Armenian Historical Museum, Erevan.*

61 *Grain jars. Pottery. Karmir-Blur. 8th century B.C. Armenian Historical Museum, Erevan.*

62 *Wine cup. Pottery. 8th century B.C. Armenian Historical Museum, Erevan.*

63 *Wine cup. Pottery. Armavir (Argishtihinili). 8th century B.C. Armenian Historical Museum, Erevan.*

64 *Cup in the shape of a rhyton. Pottery. Arin-Berd (Erebuni). 8th century B.C. Armenian Historical Museum, Erevan.*

65 *Figurine of the scorpion god. Pottery. Karmir-Blur. 8th-7th century B.C. Armenian Historical Museum, Erevan.*

66 *Fragment of a pottery jar, with decorative frieze copied from a seal. Armavir (Argishtihinili). 8th century B.C. Armenian Historical Museum, Erevan.*

67 *Pottery dishes. Armavir (Argishtihinili). 8th century B.C. Armenian Historical Museum, Erevan.*

68 *Corn jar, with lid. Red pottery. Karmir-Blur. 7th century B.C. Hermitage Museum, Leningrad.*

69 *Pottery jar. Armavir (Argishtihinili). 8th century B.C. Armenian Historical Museum, Erevan.*

70 *Bronze cauldron. Karmir-Blur. 8th century B.C. Armenian Historical Museum, Erevan.*

71 *Detail of a silver jug: hieroglyphic inscription. Karmir-Blur. 8th century B.C. Armenian Historical Museum, Erevan.*

72 *The same: detail of the handle, with a palmette ornament at the base.*

73 *The same: general view.*

74 *Door-latch from store-room, with cuneiform inscription in the name of King Rusa II. Bronze. Karmir-Blur. 7th century B.C. Hermitage Museum, Leningrad.*

75 *Fragment of a bronze cauldron. Karmir-Blur. 8th century B.C. Armenian Historical Museum, Erevan.*

76 *Bronze bells. Alişar. 7th century B.C. Hermitage Museum, Leningrad.*

77 *Horse's bit, with an inscription in the name of King Menua (810–781 B.C.). Bronze. Karmir-Blur. Armenian Historical Museum, Erevan.*

78 *Bronze fibulas. From the cemetery near Arin-Berd (Erebuni). 8th century B.C. Armenian Historical Museum, Erevan.*

79 *Pieces of harness, with an inscription in the name of King Sarduri II (760–743 B.C.): blinkers, headpiece and bridle ring. Bronze. Karmir-Blur. Hermitage Museum, Leningrad.*

80 *Fragment of a belt, with figures of Urartian divinities. Bronze. Karmir-Blur. 8th century B.C. Armenian Historical Museum, Erevan.*

81 *Fragment of a belt. Bronze. Zakim. 7th century B.C. Hermitage Museum, Leningrad.*

82 *Fragment of a bronze quiver, with iron arrowheads. Karmir-Blur. 8th century B.C. Hermitage Museum, Leningrad.*

83 *Arrowheads. On the one at the top in the centre is a cuneiform inscription in the name of King Sarduri II (760–743 B.C.). Bronze. Karmir-Blur. Hermitage Museum, Leningrad.*

84 *Fragment of a belt, with a figure of a winged griffin. Bronze. Ani-Pemsa. 8th century B.C. Armenian Historical Museum, Erevan.*

85 *Quiver, with an inscription in the name of King Sarduri II (760–743 B.C.). Bronze. Karmir-Blur. Hermitage Museum, Leningrad.*

86 *The same: detail.*

87 *Iron sword. Karmir-Blur. 8th century B.C. Armenian Historical Museum, Erevan.*

88 *Shield of King Argishti I (781–760 B.C.). Bronze. Karmir-Blur. Armenian Historical Museum, Erevan.*

89 *Shield of King Sarduri II (760–743 B.C.). Bronze. Karmir-Blur. Armenian Historical Museum, Erevan.*

90 *The same: detail.*

91 *Shield of King Argishti I (781–760 B.C). Bronze. Karmir-Blur. Hermitage Museum, Leningrad.*

92 *The same: detail.*

93 *Detail of the helmet of King Sarduri II (760–743 B.C.): chariots and horsemen. Bronze. Karmir-Blur. Hermitage Museum, Leningrad.*

94 *Detail of the helmet of King Argishti I (781–760 B.C.): genii on either side of the sacred tree. Bronze. Karmir-Blur. Hermitage Museum, Leningrad.*

95 *The same: general view.*

96 *Helmet of King Argishti II. Bronze. Karmir-Blur. Armenian Historical Museum, Erevan.*

97 *Cups with cuneiform inscriptions (names of Urartian kings). Bronze. Karmir-Blur. 8th century B.C. Hermitage Museum, Leningrad.*

98 *The same.*

99 *Winged bull. Detail from a throne. Bronze. Toprakkale. 8th–7th century B.C. Hermitage Museum, Leningrad.*

100 *Figurine of a god on a bull. Detail from a throne. Bronze. Toprakkale. 8th– 7th century B.C. Hermitage Museum, Leningrad.*

101 *Figurine of a winged lion with the head and shoulder of a man. The face is of white stone inlaid with coloured stones. Detail from a throne. Bronze with remains of gilding. Toprakkale. 8th–7th century B.C. Hermitage Museum, Leningrad.*

102 *Figurine of a winged bull. Bronze with remains of gilding. Toprakkale. 8th– 7th century B.C. Hermitage Museum, Leningrad.*

103 *Figurine of a winged woman. Cauldron handle. Bronze. Alışar. 8th century B.C. Hermitage Museum, Leningrad.*

104 *The same: rear view.*

105 *The same: three-quarters view.*

106 *Figurine of the god Teisheba (?). Bronze. Karmir-Blur. 8th century B.C. Armenian Historical Museum, Erevan.*

107 *Horse's head: an ornament from the shaft of a chariot. Bronze. Karmir- Blur. 8th century B.C. Armenian Historical Museum, Erevan.*

108 *Figurine of a bull. Cauldron handle. Bronze. Alışar. 8th century B.C. Her- mitage Museum, Leningrad.*

109 *Foot of a throne in the form of a lion's paw. Bronze. Karmir-Blur. 8th century B.C. Hermitage Museum, Leningrad.*

110 *Stone box decorated with hunting scenes. Karmir-Blur. 8th century B.C. Armenian Historical Museum, Erevan.*

111 *Stone box: side view. Karmir-Blur. 8th century B.C. Armenian Historical Museum, Erevan.*

112 *The same: lid of the box. The tree of life with a winged genius on either side.*

113   *Necklaces of cornelian, agate and faience. Karmir-Blur. 8th century B.C. Hermitage Museum, Leningrad.*

114   *Necklace and bracelet of faience. Karmir-Blur. 8th–7th century B.C. Armenian Historical Museum, Erevan.*

115   *Spoon, comb and perfume bottles. Bone. Karmir-Blur. 8th–7th century B.C. Armenian Historical Museum, Erevan.*

116   *Knife handles and object in the form of a griffin's head. Bone and horn. Karmir-Blur. 7th century B.C. Hermitage Museum, Leningrad.*

117   *Bone figurines. Karmir-Blur. 8th century B.C. Armenian Historical Museum, Erevan.*

118   *Gold bracelet. Karmir-Blur. 8th century B.C. Armenian Historical Museum, Erevan.*

119   *Ear-rings in the form of padlocks, decorated with granulation. Gold. Karmir-Blur. 8th century B.C. Armenian Historical Museum, Erevan.*

120   *Gold figurine of a lion at the end of a silver necklace. Karmir-Blur. 8th century B.C. Armenian Historical Museum, Erevan.*

121   *Fragment of a gold plaque, inlaid with turquoises, representing a lion. Karmir-Blur. 7th century B.C. Armenian Historical Museum, Erevan.*

122   *Silver medallion depicting the goddess Arubani. The goddess's head is on a gold disc welded to the medallion. Karmir-Blur. 8th century B.C. Armenian Historical Museum, Erevan.*

123   *Silver medallion depicting a sacrifice to the god Haldi. The god's head is on a gold disc welded to the medallion. Karmir-Blur. 8th century B.C. Armenian Historical Museum, Erevan.*

124   *Heads of pins. Gold. Karmir-Blur. 8th century B.C. Armenian Historical Museum, Erevan.*

125   *Lid of a vase. Silver plated with gold; the central ornament is of solid gold. Inscription with the name of King Argishti I (781–760 B.C.). Karmir-Blur. Armenian Historical Museum, Erevan.*

126 *Figurine of a divinity: restored. Wood and bronze. Karmir-Blur. 8th century B.C. Armenian Historical Museum, Erevan.*

127 *The same: unrestored. Wood. Karmir-Blur. 8th century B.C.*

128 *Head of a goddess. Wood. Karmir-Blur. 8th century B.C. Armenian Historical Museum, Erevan.*

All the photographs were taken by Gérard Bertin, Geneva.

INDEX

(The figures in italics refer to illustrations)

Achaemenid(s) 23, 71, 131, 199, 200
Adad (god) 44, 47, 67
Adduri 47
Adılcevaz 37, 38, 132, 154, 175
Agusi 83
Akurgal, E. 39
Alarodians 16
Alışar 15, *76, 103–105, 108*
Allabria 109
Alniunu 49
Altıntepe 24, 37, 127–128, 132
Alyattes, King 197
Ambaris 87
Anatolia 41
Andi 109
Ani-Pemsa *84*
Ankara Museum 24
Anzavurtepe 38
Apadana 71
Arabs 134
Aragats, Mount 21, 42
Arakelyan, B. 23
Aramaic 113, 158
Aramu the Urartian 46–51
Ararat (land) 13, 128, 198
Ararat, Mount *17*
Ararat valley 21, 23, 71
Aratsani (Arzani), River 49
Araxes, River 41, 69, 71, 72, 82, 133, 154
Arbela 134
Arda 67
Ardini *84*
Argishti I, son of Menua 15, 22, 23, 38, 68, 69, 70, 71, 72, 81, 83, 84, 115, 128, 153, 156, 159, 160, 174, 199, *38, 88, 91–92, 94–95, 125*
Argishti II, son of Rusa 37, 38, 125–129, 131, 132, 139, 153, 159, *96*
Argishtihinili (Armavir) 24, 72, 82, 154, *59, 63, 66, 67, 69*
Arin-Berd 22, 69, 127, *1–13, 38, 64, 78*

Armali 47
Armavir 21, 23, 154, *59, 63, 66, 67, 69*
Armavir-Blur 23
Arme 82, 199
Armenia(n) 13, 14, 21–24, 39, 41–42, 43, 44, 48, 50, 51, 82, 128, 135, 199, 200
Armenian Academy of Science 22, 23, 135
Armenian Historical Museum 116, 135, 174, *8–13, 16, 34–45, 47–48, 51, 54, 55, 58–67, 69–73, 75, 77, 78, 80, 84, 87–90, 96, 106, 107, 110–112, 114–115, 117–128*
Armenian Museum of Wine-making 180
Armina 200
Arpad 83
Artik 42
Artsibi (horse) 156
Arubani (goddess) 66, 114, 116, 175, *122*
Arutyunyan, N. V. 39
Aryan 16
Arzani (Aratsani), River 49
Arzashku 46, 47
Ashchenaz (Scythians) 198
Ashguzaya (Scythians) 129
Ashur (god) 44, 88, 125, 196
Ashurbanipal 18, 134, 195, 196, 200
Ashur-bel-dan 87
Ashurnasirpal II 15, 45, 70
Ashur-risua 87
Ashur-uballit 197
Asia Minor 39, 42, 67, 68, 81, 175, 176
Asia, Western 16, 41, 45, 51, 67, 71, 81, 82, 85, 129, 130, 156, 174, 175, 197, 198
Assur (city) 43, 88, 125, 175, 197, 198
Assyria(n) 13, 15, 16, 17, 18, 19, 39, 42, 43–51, 65, 66,

67, 68, 70, 81, 82, 83, 84, 86–88, 109–116, 125–129, 131, 133, 134, 137–138, 156, 158, 175, 193, *195, 196, 197–199, 43, 45*
Austria 17
Aygestan 17
Aza 88, 153, 154

Babylonia(n) 16, 39, 126, 197, 198, 200, *43*
Bagmashtu (goddess) 113, 114
Balawat 18, 45–48
Balkan, K. 38
Barnett, R. D. 17, 19, 39
Batu 160
Bavian, Mount 127
Behistun 200
Belck, W. 19
Bel-Iddin 109
Berlin Museums 17, 20, 199
Biaini(li) 50, 51, 69, 85
Bible 13
Bilgiç, E. 37
Bit-Akitu (Uruk) 136
Bit-Hanunia 198
Black Sea 44
British Museum 17, 18, 19, 37, 116
Brosset, M. 16
Burney, C. A. 24, 38
Byzantium 16

Carchemish 197
Caucasus 39, 42, 85, 129, 130, 154, 176, 199, 200
Chorokh (Çoruh), River 43
Cimmerians 85, 87, 129, 130
Clayton, Capt. E. 19
Constantinople 17, 18
Culamerk 14
Cyaxares 197

Çavuştepe 38
Çoruh (Chorokh), River 43

Daian-Ashur 49
Daiani 43, 47
Daiukku 88
Darius I 200
Darius II 200
David 23, 24
Devgants, S. 17, 18
Diyarbakır 125
Dnieper, River 130, 176
Dur-Sharrukin 88, 110, 125
Dyakonov, I. M. 39

Echmiadzin 135, 139
Egypt(ian) 86, 127, 176, 197, *43*
Elamites 134, 200
Erciş 126
Erebuni (Arin-Berd) 22–23, 24, 37, 69–72, 82, 85, 154, 160, 178, 180, 200, *1–13, 38, 64, 78*
Erevan 22, 133, 135, 140, 174
Erimena, King 37, 131, 195, 196, 197, *35*
Eritna 47
Erzen, A. 37, 38
Erzincan 24, 127
Esarhaddon, King 128, 129
Etruscan(s) 39, 68
Euphrates, River 68, 82, 83, 130

Flandin, E. 112
French Asiatic Society 14
Friedrich, J. 39

Gabbuana-Ashur 87
Georgian Museum, Tbilisi 116
Gilurani 160
Gimirraya (Cimmerians) 129
Goetze, A. 39
Gordion 81
Greece, Greek 39, 68, 81
Gurgum 83

Habhu 113, 156
Habur, River 42
Haldi (god) 66, 70, 84, 85, 111, 112, 113, 114, 115, 125, 131, 139, 153, 159, 160, 173, 175, *13, 123*
Haldi (town) 67
Halittu 130
Halys, River 197
Hamath 88
Hamburg Museum 20
Harda 125
Harmakku 88
Harran 197
Hasanlu 113
Hatti 69, 130
Hebat (goddess) 67
Hermitage Museum, Leningrad 15, 17, 22, 135, *14, 15, 25, 29, 46, 49, 50, 52, 53, 56, 57, 68, 74, 76, 79, 81–83, 85–86, 91–95, 97–105, 108, 109, 113, 116*
Herodotus 16, 197
Hittite(s) 16, 42, 48, 72, 128
Horhor 68, 69, 128
Huba (goddess) 67
Hubha 109
Hubushkia 130
Hulin, P. 24
Hurrian(s) 16, 41, 42, 48, 67, 69, 81

Ildaruni, River 139
Imgur-Enlil 45
Institute of Archaeology, London 38
Iran(ian) 15, 114, 131, 132, 198, 199, 200
Ishdi-Harran 129
Ishpaka 129
Ishpilini 160
Ishpuini, King 50, 65, 115, 156
Istanbul Museum 15, 16
Italy 81
Iuarsha (god) 70

Iubsha (Iuarsha) 70
Ivanovsky, A. 21

Jeremiah 198

Kalhu 70, 82, 86, 88, 132, 198
Kamo 85
Karas 37, 47
Karmir-Blur 22, 85, 115, 116, 133, 135–140, 153–160, 173–180, 193, 197, 199, *16–37, 39–43, 45–58, 60, 61, 65, 68, 70–75, 77, 79, 80, 82, 83, 85–98, 106, 107, 109–128*
Kayalidere 38
Kefkalesi 37, 132
Kelermes 176, 177
Kelishin 50
Khorenatsi, Moses 13, 14
Khorsabad 15
Kirovakan 42
König, F. W. 39
Kumanu 67
Kummuh 83, 126
Kurdistan, Kurds 15, 41, 127
Kuturlini 139
Kuyunjik 87

Lake, K. 20
Lamassu 112
Layard, Sir Henry 17, 18
Lchashen 42
Lehmann-Haupt, C. F. 19
Leningrad 17
Lloyd, Seton 38
London 17, 18
London University 38
Longpérier, Prévost de 16
Louvre 88, 109, 111, 113, 114, 115, 116
Lutipri, King 49
Lydian 197

Madyes 197
Maki 130
Mannai, Mannaean 88, 109, 129, 130, 198
Manu 132
Marr, N. Y. 20
Martirosyan, A. 23, *59*
Massoretic writers 13
Mazgerd 130
Medes, Median 130, 131, 178, 196–197, 198, 199
Mediterranean 39, 68, 81, 130, 175
Melgunov 177
Melikishvili, G. A. 39
Melita 69, 83
Menua, King 14, 15, 23, 38, 65, 68, 153, 156, *77*
Menuahinili 21
Meshchaninov, I. 39
Mesopotamia 15, 20, 41, 68, 136, 138
Metatti 109
Meyer, G. R. 20, 39
Mheri-Dur 66, 67
Minua (Menua), King 65
Minni (Mannai) 198
Mitanni(an) 42
Musasir 67, 84, 87, 88, 111, 112, 113, 114, 116, 125, 156, 174
Mushkini 130
Muş 38

Nabu-li 87
Nabupalasar 197, 198
Nabu-Shalimshunu 88
Nairi, Land of 43, 44, 46, 49, 50, 51, 111
Nairi, Sea of (Lake Van) 45, 46, 51
Naqsh-i Rustam 200
Naragu 87
Nikolsky, M. V. 21
Nimrud 15, 70
Nineveh 18, 45, 86, 87, 109, 126, 127, 129, 134, 158, 197, 198, 200

Nor-Bayazed 85

Oganesyan, K. L. 23, *8*
Old Testament 13, 128
Orbeli, I. A. 20
Osetia 199

Öğün, B. 37
Özgüç, T. 37

Palestine 86, 126
Pallottino, M. 39
Parda 109
Paris 15
Partatua (Protothyes) 129, 197
Patkanov, K. 17
Patnos 38
Persepolis 200
Persia: *see* Iran
Phrygia 81
Piotrovsky, B. B. 17, 22
Protothyes (Partatua) 197
Pushkin Museum, Moscow 23

Qumran scrolls 13

Rassam, Hormuzd 18, 19
Raynolds, D. 19
Razdan, River 135, 139
Rhodes 176
Rusa I, son of Sarduri 84–88, 109, 111, 114, 115, 116, 125, 153, 159, 160
Rusa II, son of Argishti 20, 22, 37, 38, 129–130, 131, 132, 133, 134, 135, 139, 153, 154, 195, 196, 197, *74*
Rusa III, son of Erimena 37, 131, 157, 195, 196, 197
Rusa IV, son of Rusa 157, 197
Rusahinili see Toprakkale
Russian Archaeological Society 20

Sahand, Mount 109
St Petersburg 15
St Petersburg University 17
Samiram, Sammuramat, Queen 13, 14
Sarduri I, son of Lutipri 49, 50, 65
Sarduri II, son of Argishti 20, 23, 69, 81–83, 84, 85, 153, 156, 159, 160, 199, *79*, *83*, *85*, *86*, *89–90*, *93*
Sarduri III, son of Rusa 38, 134, 195, 196, 197
Sarduri IV, son of Sarduri 196, 197
Sarduri, son of Ishpuini 115
Sargon, King 15, 67, 68, 86–88, 109–116, 125–126, 137, 156, 174
Sargonids 175
Sassanian 15
Schulz, F. E. 14, 15, 16
Scythian(s) 39, 129, 130, 176, 177, 178, 196, 197, 198, 199
Semiramis, Queen 13
Semitic 16
Sennacherib, King 86, 126–127, 128, 129, 158
Sevan, Lake 21, 42, 69, 82, 85, 153
Shabaka, Pharaoh 86, 158
Shalmaneser I 43
Shalmaneser III 18, 45–49
Shalmaneser V 86
Shamash (god) 44, 67, 129
Shamshi-ilu 68
Shivini (god) 66, 67, 173, 175
Shupria 128, 129
Siduri (Sarduri), King 49, 51
Sin-ahi-usur 110
Sohmet (goddess) 176, *44*
Stasov, V. V. 16
Subi 110
Sugunia 46
Susa 134

Susi temple 70, 127, 131, 153, *6*
Syria 42, 69, 72, 83, 86, 126, 176

Tabal 87, 111
Tabshar-Ashur 88
Tas (Mount Bavian) 127
Tashburun 21
Tbilisi (Tiflis) 16, 116
Teisheba (god) 37, 66–67, 85, 116, 126, 132, 153, 173, 174
Teishebaini (Karmir-Blur) 22, 23, 24, 85, 115, 130, 133, 135–140, 153–160, 173–180, 193, 196, 197, 199, 200
Teshub (god) 67
Teuman, King 134
Teushpa 129
Tiglath-Pileser I 43, 47
Tiglath-Pileser III 82–83, 86, 116
Tigris, River 43, 82, 112, 125
Til-Barsip 68
Titumnia 126
Tli 199
Toprakkale 17, 19, 20, 37, 39, 85, 126, 130–131, 132,

178, 195, 196, 199, *14*, *15*, *99–102*
Transcaucasia 21, 22, 23, 39, 69, 72, 85, 130, 133, 160, 175, 176, 177, 199
Trialeti 42
Tsolakert 21
Tsovinar 86
Tsupani 69
Tukulti-Ninurta I 43
Turkey 11, 14, 24, 37–38, 39
Turushpa (Tushpa) 83
Tushpa 49, 65–66, 67, 82, 83, 87, 111, 126, 130, 195
Tushpuea (goddess) 67
Tutankhamen 114

Uasi 87
Uaush (Mount Sahand) 109, 110
Uelikuhi 85
Uishdish 110
Ulhu 110
Ullusunu 88
Umeshini 139–140
Umman-Manda 196
Uppahir-Bel 86
Urashtu 198, 200
Urmia, Lake 42, 72, 82, 84, 88, 110, 111, 113

Ursa (Rusa), King 115, 125
Uruatri 43, 45, 51
Uruk 136
Urzana 84, 87, 111

Van (town site) 14, 15, 16, 17, 18, 19, 20, 37, 39, 66, 68, 82, 83, 85, 116, 127, 156, 200
Van, Kingdom of 16, 39, 51, 81, 84, 125, 131, 195, 200
Van, Lake 11, 13, 14, 18, 24, 37, 38, 41, 43, 45, 46, 47, 48, 49, 50, 51, 87, 111, 126, 127, 129, 130, 199
Verkhnaya Rutkha 199

Xerxes 16, 200

Zab, River 43, 88
Zakim *81*
Zedekiah, King 198
Zeyva 199
Zikirtu 109
Zimzim-Magara 17
Ziwiye treasure 177, 198
Zvarthnots 139

Printed in Switzerland

THE TEXT AND ILLUSTRATIONS
IN THIS VOLUME WERE PRINTED
ON THE PRESSES OF NAGEL
PUBLISHERS IN GENEVA

FINISHED IN JANUARY 1969
BINDING BY NAGEL PUBLISHERS,
GENEVA

PLATES ENGRAVED BY CLICHÉS UNION, PARIS

LEGAL DEPOSIT No 467

PRINTED IN SWITZERLAND

913.3
Piotrovsky, Boris B.
The ancient civilization of Urartu.

10-71

0   250 Miles

DIAUEHI

TABAL

U R A

ALZI
ENZITE

Uai

Arzani

KUMMUH

Melita

Bit-Zamani

Markasi

(Euphrates)

Nasibina

Til-Barsip

Harran

Carchemish

A   S   S

Arpad

Purattu